20

THE OPEN MEDIA PAMPHLET SERIES

THE OPEN MEDIA PAMPHLET SERIES

Islands of Resistance
Puerto Rico, Vieques, and U.S. Policy

MARIO MURILLO

Open Media Pamplet Series Editor:
Greg Ruggiero

SEVEN STORIES PRESS / New York

A Seven Stories Press First Edition,
published in association with Open Media.

Murillo, Mario (Mario A.)
        Islands of resistance: Puerto Rico, Vieques, and U.S. policy /
Mario Murillo.-1st ed.
        p. cm. - (Open media pamphlet series)
        ISBN 1-58322-080-1 (pbk.)
        1. United States-Foreign relations—Puerto Rico. 2. Puerto
Rico—Foreign relations—United States. 3. United States—Foreign
relations—1993–   4. Puerto Rico—History—Autonomy and independence movements. 5. Vieques Island (P.R.)—History—20th century.
6. Ordnance testing—Puerto Rico—Vieques Island—History—20th century. 7. United States—Foreign relations—20th century. I. Series.
E183.8.P9 M87 2001
325'.37307295-dc21   00-050510

Book design by Cindy LaBreacht

9 8 7 6 5 4 3 2 1

Printed in Canada.

SPECIAL THANKS TO: Megan Costello, who researched and helped write the section on media coverage; Robert Rabin of the Committee for the Rescue and Development of Vieques, for providing me and many others with key information about the struggle against the navy; John Lindsay Poland of the Fellowship of Reconciliation Task Force on Latin America and the Caribbean; Ben "the Pen" Ramos; Esperanza Martell of Pro Libertad, for her tireless work for the community; Dr. Emilio Pantojas and Dr. Jorge Rodriguez Beruf of the University of Puerto Rico, Rio Piedras; and Maria Victoria Maldonado for her opinions and extraordinary patience.

"We have not come to make war upon the people of a country that for centuries has been oppressed, but on the contrary, to bring you protection... to promote your prosperity, and to bestow upon you the immunities and blessings of the liberal institutions of our government."

—General Nelson Miles
July 25, 1898
Guánica, Puerto Rico

"Under the Constitution of the United States, no power is given to the federal government to acquire territory to be governed permanently as colonies."

—From the *Congressional Record*
55th Congress, first session, February 6, 1899

ISLANDS OF RESISTANCE

INTRODUCTION

In the early 1990s, Puerto Rican activists representing the island's three main political currents kept pointing to 1998 as a milestone year that was going to put Puerto Rico back on the map of U.S. political consciousness. Much as 1992 had been a rallying cry for the indigenous rights movement across the Americas, when five hundred years of resistance was to be celebrated against the backdrop of the countless official commemorations of the European encroachment on the Western Hemisphere, 1998 was being anticipated as a pivotal moment for the Puerto Rican movement toward self-determination, to rekindle the spark that had dwindled in the infant days of the post–Cold War era.

From the many organizations doing tireless work to free the jailed Puerto Rican nationalists, to the many pro-independence and pro-statehood groups that had been mobilizing around the status issue for years, to the many U.S.-based activists who emerged from the radical movements of the 1960s and '70s, Puerto Ricans on the island and in the United States were looking forward to 1998 as a watershed opportunity in their struggle to alter the colonial relationship with the United States that the island has endured for the entire 20th century.

The reasons for this universal enthusiasm were simple, if not obvious. Centennial moments don't come around too often, and 1998 marked the 100th anniversary of the U.S. invasion of Puerto Rico in the final stages of the Spanish-American War. It was on July 25, 1898, that the U.S. Marines landed in the southern coastal town of Guánica at the end of the Spanish-American War, an event that would forever alter the history of Puerto Rico. Depending on one's political perspective, this date marks either the beginning of a century of U.S. colonial domination of Puerto Rican society or the beginning of a unique relationship that has reaped tremendous benefits for the Caribbean island of 4 million people. The thinking of Puerto Ricans was that this centennial commemoration, however artificial, would provide an opportunity to either denounce the colonialist policies of the United States regarding Puerto Rico or embrace the close relationship that has existed between the two nations since they were unceremoniously joined by U.S. military intervention at the turn of the nineteenth century.

For the pro-statehood movement, the centennial was a time to celebrate the rewards of a 100-year connection to the United States that has made Puerto Rico the shining star in the Caribbean. At the same time, according to the annexationist pro-statehooders, this connection was still incomplete, and indeed remained a colonial one that needed to be solidified permanently by an act of Congress that would make Puerto Rico the 51st state of the United States. The year 1998 symbolized "the celebration of our people of one hundred years of union with the United States, a date that one hundred years ago brought the stars and stripes into Puerto Rico with an accompanying promise of democracy and equal rights for our people," said pro-statehood Governor Pedro Roselló on the eve of the commemoration.[1]

For the proponents of the Free Associated State, or the so-called commonwealth status, led by the Popular Democratic Party (PPD), 1998 was seen as a time to celebrate the virtues of a U.S.-imposed citizenship that had reaped countless benefits for a people that still took pride in its Latino-Caribbean roots and culture. To describe the relationship between the United States and Puerto Rico as colonial, the *populares* argue, is to ignore the autonomy that island residents and their government enjoy, while rejecting the freedom islanders maintain as U.S. citizens. In other words, for the defenders of the status quo, 1998 was a time to once again embrace the best of both worlds, which for years had been in their eyes unjustifiably characterized as a colonial limbo.

For the many different sectors of Puerto Rico's independence movement, 1998 was a time to reflect on the U.S. invasion of one hundred years earlier, while at the same time celebrating a tradition of resistance that has made heroes of the likes of Don Pedro Albizu Campos, Eugenio Maria de Hostos, and Ramón Emeterio Betances, to name a few. The *independentistas*, forever ostracized and persecuted for their firm belief that Puerto Rico is a nation in and of itself and that the United States has no right or jurisdiction over the island, thought that 1998 would force the powers in Washington to seriously address the island's status question, and that once all options were deemed unattainable, independence would be the inevitable outcome. "When one hundred years passes by and the United States realizes the fact that it is the last colonial power in the world, a number of people will be asking what should happen to Puerto Rico," said Puerto Rican senator Rubén Berríos Martinez of the Puerto Rican Independence Party (PIP).[2]

As it turned out, despite the hype and anticipation, 1998 came and went, and very little, if anything, changed. When the year so much attention was going to be directed toward Puerto Rico had passed, the island's status had not come any closer to being resolved, the internal divisions in Puerto Rico remained, and the U.S. political establishment continued its unwillingness to resolve the colonial situation of Puerto Rico. In fact, with the exception of a brief congressional debate over a piece of legislation aimed at addressing the status question, very few people asked the question, What should be done with Puerto Rico? Once again, the Puerto Rico question fell into the media's silent abyss and was received with the collective indifference that has characterized North American attitudes towards Puerto Rico and its people for generations.

In 1998 I made several visits down to the island, having made a commitment a few years earlier to do something special for Puerto Rico on its momentous anniversary. I wanted to mark the moment with a personal reflection about what Puerto Rico meant to me, both as a U.S.-born Puerto Rican who had always felt a close connection to the people's struggle for self-determination and as an independent radio journalist who for years had covered the many social, economic, and political developments of the entire Latin American and Caribbean region. My reports and radio documentaries looked closely at the imperial enterprise of the United States in Latin America and the Caribbean, almost always with a particular focus on how the United States utilized its immense war machine throughout the Western Hemisphere to protect its own economic and strategic interests. Puerto Rico was perhaps the best example of this enterprise.

I thought back to some of my earliest family visits to Puerto Rico when I was maybe six or seven years old, getting to know the wonders of the island my mother once called home. These are some of the finest memories I have: the sounds of the *coquí* in the backyard, the *gallos* reminding us it was time to shake the sleep from our eyes, the friendly crowds in the central plaza in the town of Moca, where my mother and her ten brothers and sisters were born and raised, the whiff of the sugarcane fields and the orange groves, the large chicken coops that my late uncle Rate operated outside of Aguadilla—and how my cousins and I used to have contests every morning to see who would pull out the most eggs. I am certain thousands of Puerto Ricans experience a similar nostalgia when reflecting on their first visits to "La Isla del Encanto."

I also remember driving through the former Ramey Air Base in the western end of the island for the first time, completely awed by the immaculate landscape and charming little homes of the U.S. servicemen. The resources at their disposal were quite impressive, making a young child like myself even think that perhaps one day it might be a good job to become a navy man. At the time it hadn't dawned on me that these U.S. military personnel had not been invited to the island.

It was actually in late 1993 during a visit to Panama that I first began to formulate concrete thoughts about producing something for the 1998 centennial of the United States in Puerto Rico. I was in Panama accompanying a delegation sponsored by the Fellowship of Reconciliation Task Force on Latin America and the Caribbean (FORTFLAC), an organization that for years had been doing extensive work on the demilitarization of Panama.[3] Specifically, the delegation went down to monitor the process of U.S. military withdrawal from the fourteen bases in Panama that was to be completed on December

31, 1999, as part of the Carter-Torrijos Panama Canal Treaties, signed in 1977. In its work, FOR-TFLAC was concerned about U.S. compliance with the accords, which included the cleanup process of the former bases, referred to as the "reverted areas." FOR-TFLAC had documented years of environmental negligence by the military in Panama, and they wanted to put pressure on Pentagon officials to make certain the United States would clean up the areas upon their departure. The issues of economic conversion and development of the areas were also a major cause for concern, both for FOR-TFLAC, and more importantly, for the many Panamanian organizations that had been struggling for years to get the United States out of Panama and reclaim sovereignty over the Panama Canal.[4]

Although these issues gained some attention in the United States toward the end of 1999 when the process was finally completed and the canal was returned to Panama, in late 1993 it was perhaps the last thing on people's minds. After all, once the U.S. military invaded Panama in December 1989, ostensibly to arrest General Manuel Antonio Noriega and decimate the Panamanian Defense Force, the U.S. media had pretty much forgotten about Panama, its people, and the fulfillment of the canal treaty. This indifference is not unlike the indifference we see again and again with respect to Puerto Rico, or any of a number of spots around the region and indeed the world where the U.S. military has maintained a presence for so many years with very little accountability.

So naturally, I began thinking about Puerto Rico while interviewing U.S. military officials, the U.S. Ambassador, Panamanian elected officials, labor leaders, and peace activists during my visit to Panama in 1993.[5]

I remember a conversation I had with one extremely dedicated and passionate Panamanian activist, Nicolasa Terreros of the human rights organization Service for Peace and Justice, where she described to me her disgust with seeing the U.S. stars and stripes flying alongside her country's flag everywhere she went in the Canal Zone, and retold the infamous events of 1964 when U.S. soldiers opened fire on Panamanian students who had the audacity to raise their flag at Balboa High School. I told her that I had experienced some of these same feelings on just about every one of my visits to Puerto Rico, where even at McDonald's the U.S. flag flies alongside Puerto Rico's, if not above it. The parallels between Panama and Puerto Rico were striking.

After several visits to Puerto Rico in 1998, the end result was a two-part radio documentary that I produced for Pacifica Radio, which focused on the military occupation of Puerto Rico, and in particular the almost sixty-year struggle of the people of Vieques, a small island six miles off the eastern coast of mainland Puerto Rico.[6] For generations Vieques inhabitants have rallied together to demand an end to U.S. colonialism, whether they were pro-statehood or pro-independence. How was it possible that a civilian population of less than 10,000, many of whom were forcibly displaced from their original land by the U.S. Navy, was forced to live surrounded by a naval bombing range and munitions storage facility? Why was it that the voices of these people who have endured almost year-round bombing tests were never heard outside Puerto Rico? I thought that if the centennial were going to be adequately examined, Vieques would be a very good starting point. In my visits to Puerto Rico in 1998, I talked to U.S.

Navy personnel, with Vieques locals, with fishermen, with politicians, and with others who lived on the island. I also talked to a number of political leaders, including the top representatives of the three main parties on the island.

The radio documentary aired with very little fanfare. While a number of people applauded the effort, I was struck most by the comments of a good friend and astute political analyst, Puerto Rican attorney and activist Howard Jordan, who jokingly said to me, "Hey, why are you dealing with Vieques now? That's a dead issue. Nobody wants to hear about Vieques anymore." Of course, he was being facetious. But his words struck me more profoundly than any of the other compliments or critiques I received in the wake of the initial broadcast. What Howard was saying was true. Nobody wanted to hear about Vieques. Ultimately, my radio documentary fell on deaf ears, as did much of the other hoopla that went on in 1998 around the centennial commemorations. With very few exceptions, the U.S. public, even within progressive circles, was once again not quite ready to be bothered by the Puerto Rico question.

Ironically in 1999, people were forced to pay attention to Puerto Rico once again, mainly because of two events that took place within several months of each other that exposed the nature of Washington's control over Puerto Rico and its people. The first was the death of Puerto Rican security guard David Sanes Rodriguez on April 19, 1999, who was killed by an "errant" 500-pound bomb that was part of one of the navy's ongoing war games in Vieques. His death sparked a series of massive mobilizations in Vieques, on the mainland of Puerto Rico, and in cities across the United States, demanding that the U.S.

Navy get out of Vieques once and for all. Unlike the protests and rallies commemorating the 1998 centennial, this movement was not going to be ignored.

The other major event of 1999 was the release from prison of 11 Puerto Rican nationalists, members of the radical Armed Forces of National Liberation (FALN) jailed for their pro-independence activities in the late 1970s and early '80s.[7] Their release came after President Bill Clinton granted limited clemency to eleven of the sixteen political prisoners who had served almost twenty years of their disproportionately long sentences. While this was the result of years of pressure by grassroots political and human rights groups in Puerto Rico, the United States, and other countries around the world, the president's act was decried by conservative and liberal politicians alike as being nothing but political opportunism, given that his wife, Hillary Rodham Clinton, was running for senate in New York State, a major base of Puerto Rican politics. Perhaps it was not surprising that even the first lady tried to distance herself from her husband's decision, something that came back to haunt her when she was immediately scolded by many of her Puerto Rican political supporters in New York. For the most part, the focus of attention in the media was the political grandstanding that took place after the announced clemency. Nevertheless, the release of the nationalists drew attention for a brief moment to the many injustices carried out by U.S. federal and Puerto Rican colonial authorities against the Puerto Rican independence movement, injustices that were brought to light in May 2000, when FBI director Louis Freeh made public thousands of formerly classified files the agency maintained on leaders of the Puerto Rican independence sector, a disclo-

sure that was demanded by U.S. representative Jose Serrano of New York, one of three Puerto Ricans in Congress.[8]

These two events, the tragic death of David Sanes and
the release of the eleven *independentistas*, transformed
a movement in that they brought together for the first
time so many different political forces and interests, all
calling for some fundamental changes in the relationship
between Washington and Puerto Rico. They gave the U.S.
public a brief glimpse of the passions of a people who
refuse to relinquish their history, their culture, their language, and their national pride, despite over 100 years of
colonial subjugation.

Resistance is manifested in the people of Vieques,
who despite great risks have not rested since the death of
David Sanes, and are committed to continue protesting
until the navy finally leaves the island municipality
known as *La Isla Nena*. Resistance is manifested in the
groups who continue struggling for the release of the
remaining Puerto Rican political prisoners who were
either not part of the President's clemency deal or refused
to accept it on principle. And finally, it is manifested in
the tens of thousands of people fighting within official and
nonofficial circles for a just, democratic, and acceptable
resolution to the status question, which is no closer to
being resolved today than it was when General Nelson
Miles first landed on Puerto Rico in 1898.

IT ALL BEGAN WITH A MILITARY INVASION

How and where does one begin telling the story of Puerto
Rico? Do we go back to the end of the fifteenth century,
when Christopher Columbus set out on his famous jour-
ney that led to the clash between Europe and the Amer-

icas? Do we begin with the early stages of that clash, when Columbus landed on the island of Borinquen on November 19, 1493, beginning the European onslaught that within one generation decimated more than two-thirds of the native Taíno population?[9]

Do we examine the 400 years of European colonialism on the island, a greedy enterprise of the Spanish crown that resulted not only in the complete extraction of the island's gold and other mineral resources by the middle of the sixteenth century but also led to the establishment of one of the most brutal systems of subservience and exploitation of both indigenous and African populations in the Americas?

Perhaps it would be more useful to begin the story by looking at one of the most profound acts of resistance to Spanish power, when over 500 Puerto Rican patriots organized to rid themselves of the colonial cloak that was stifling all forms of social and economic development on the island. This act of rebellion, known as El Grito de Lares, occurred on September 23, 1868, about thirty years before Spain's grip on the island was finally loosened. Led by day laborers, farmers, and former slaves, the rebels of El Grito de Lares declared an independent Puerto Rican nation, demanding that the Spanish recognize the new republic. However, without masses of the population stepping in to back them up, Spain repressed the independence movement, forcing the people to wait yet again for its self-determination. Nevertheless, to this day, Lares serves as a symbol of the centuries-long resistance of the Puerto Rican people to colonialism.

Indeed the story of contemporary Puerto Rico begins in 1898, when it was expected that self-determination was finally going to be achieved as one of the fruits of United States intervention during the Spanish-American War. In fact the arrival of General Nelson Miles' forces in the southern port of Guánica on July 25 of that year was embraced by many Puerto Ricans as the first step toward the island's eventual independence. Therefore, to understand the significance of the never-ending debate over the island's political status, as well as to place the many manifestations against United States colonialism over the years into a proper context, it makes sense to begin with a look at how the United States wrestled control of the island from the fading Spanish empire at the turn of the last century. The popular resistance to the U.S. Navy on the island of Vieques and elsewhere in Puerto Rico today, as well as the struggle waged by the Puerto Rican nationalists released from prison by President Clinton in August 1999, cannot be understood without a firm understanding of this tumultuous history.

The United States had always looked at Puerto Rico and Cuba as essential components for the protection of its growing empire.[10] As far back as 1823, when U.S. president Monroe issued his Monroe Doctrine, preoccupation with Cuba and the Caribbean was already evident. Once the westward expansion in the continental United States was completed in the wake of the war with Mexico in 1848, military planners and policymakers in Washington began to focus even more attention on the Caribbean, the manifest destiny concept now by necessity being applied to the south. The seeds of this policy were planted by President Franklin Pierce's ambassador to Spain, who issued a document in the 1850s that stated if Washington couldn't obtain Cuba by peaceful means, then "we shall be justified in wresting it from Spain if we possess the power (to do so)."[11] This period, often characterized in U.S. textbooks as one where the United States took an isolationist approach to international relations, was in fact a period of intense expansionism. Washington viewed any European involvement in the Western Hemisphere as interference in its own backyard, and deemed such meddling as a direct threat to national security. Naturally, the United States was recovering from its own period of major internal strife, that of the Civil War, and began to flex its muscles to demonstrate military, and in particular naval, superiority in the region. In those days of coal-burning ships, the only way to achieve this superiority was to maintain secure international coaling ports, hence the interest in the Philippines, Hawaii, and Guam in the Pacific, and Cuba and Puerto Rico in the Caribbean.[12] The claims made by the Pentagon, the White House, and many members of congress in 1999 and 2000 that the Naval bombing range in Vieques is absolutely necessary in order to maintain military readiness for U.S. forces around the world, therefore, are not new, and have as their origins those initial designs on the Caribbean that were shaped by people like former secretary of the navy Theodore Roosevelt back in the 1890s, as well as many before him.[13]

Cuba was seen as the main target of U.S. expansionism. The many demands from Cubans on the island calling for the United States to annex Cuba from Spain generated considerable enthusiasm in the U.S. press. Washington and its allies in the yellow newspapers of the time, Hearst's *New York Journal* to name one, carefully orchestrated tensions with Spain in its effort to win the hearts and minds of the U.S. public and get them ready for war. This was taking place within the backdrop of ongoing negotiations between President William McKinley and the Spanish government, ostensibly to resolve the autonomy issue with regard to Cuba. While it was always presented in the press as a case of the United States coming to the defense of the poor Cubans, who were struggling for their freedom against a tyrannical, colonial power, much like today's media coverage of Latin America, very little was said about the deeper economic and military intentions of the government in Washington.

Tensions increased between Spain and the United States just as Cuba and Puerto Rico were being groomed for limited autonomy. Despite the signing of the Autonomic Charters for Cuba and Puerto Rico on November 25, 1897, which actually did little to change the conditions of the people on either island,[14] the United States dispatched the battleship Maine to Havana to protect the lives of American citizens and property (even back then this was seen as the most justifiable manner in which to sell U.S. military intervention in the Americas to the U.S. public). On February 15, 1898, the *Maine* exploded in Havana Bay, killing 260 crewmembers and wounding dozens of others. It proved to be the final nail in the coffin that carried U.S.-Spanish relations, a nail the U.S. press was quite ready to begin hammering with the slogan "Remember the *Maine*." Despite little evidence linking Spain to the explosion, it was presented to everyone as enough cause to get the United States into a war with Spain, "that splendid little war" that eventually led to the independence of Cuba, albeit as a protectorate of the United States, and the continued domination of Puerto Rico by a foreign power.[15]

While Cuba was the main focus of President McKinley and his advisers, even before it was clear that Cuba would eventually become independent, it was already on the minds of the hawks of the Spanish-American War that Puerto Rico would not be surrendered. Puerto Rico was going to be Washington's war booty. So it was that when General Miles landed on Guánica with his 3,000 men, the outcome of the war had already been decided. Historians point out that to a certain extent, General Miles decided to militarily invade Puerto Rico primarily because he wanted to make up for the losses his men suffered when he invaded Cuba a few weeks earlier. More importantly, he knew he would find little resistance on the island because most Puerto Ricans welcomed the U.S. forces, thinking that they were finally going to gain their freedom from Spain.[16] What essentially could have been handled on the diplomatic front, therefore, was carried out by the navy. The U.S. flag was now hoisted upon Puerto Rico, and thus began a century of U.S. political, economic, cultural, and military domination of the island.

ONCE A COLONY, ALWAYS A COLONY

Despite the enthusiasm with which many on the island greeted the U.S. military at the outset, concerns quickly began to mount when it became apparent that notwithstanding the ideals of the U.S. Constitution, the Declaration of Independence, and the promises made by General Miles, liberty was not forthcoming for Borinquen.[17] On August 12, 1898, the Treaty of Paris officially ceded Puerto Rico to the United States, while Cuba, its independence movement stronger than Puerto Rico's, gained its independence. Within eighteen months, after officials in Washington failed to act on petitions from prominent Puerto Ricans demanding an end to the military government, the U.S. Congress passed the Foraker Act, thus making Puerto Rico the first unincorporated territory of the United States. Unlike other territories that had been annexed by the U.S., Puerto Rico was never given a stated promise that it would eventually become a state of the union. The Foraker Act tried to legitimize United States colonial rule over the island by making Puerto Ricans citizens of Puerto Rico, not of the United States, leaving them without any representation in the U.S. Congress.

Against the will of the Puerto Rican people, this colonial arrangement remained the same for over fifteen years. While frustrating the island's political vanguard, these first few years of U.S. control were also important in that they allowed the United States to consolidate the foundations of its economic domination of the island. The U.S. sugar industry and its friends in Washington transformed Puerto Rico's economy. The colonial economy, established prior to the Spanish defeat in 1898, for decades had already been seen as a system that could be exploited by the United States. Now, with Washington firmly in control, this process accelerated, for the most part benefiting the U.S. sugar refineries as well as the U.S. market, while limiting the capacity of Puerto Rican growers from competing in the global market. Conditions improved somewhat for many Puerto Ricans, as the United States invested millions of dollars improving infrastructure on the island. Yet illiteracy, unemployment, and personal income saw very little change during the first generations of U.S. control. Even later, when Puerto Rico underwent a process of rapid industrialization, unemployment did not see any marked improvements in the general population.[18]

Meanwhile, any discussion of Puerto Rico in the U.S. Congress, news media, and in academic circles was riddled with racist language that once again supported the myth of Anglo-American superiority over Puerto Ricans, and denigrated the Afro-indigenous-Spanish cultural and racial mix that existed on the island, presenting to the U.S. public an image of a people incapable of self-governance. As Jose Trias Monge points out in his book *Puerto Rico: The Trials of the Oldest Colony in the World*, academics such as Simeon E. Baldwin of Yale Law School expressed the view of the day when he wrote: "Our Constitution was made by a civilized and educated people. It provides guaranties of personal security which seem ill-adapted to the conditions of society that prevail in many parts of our new possessions. To give...the ignorant and lawless brigands that infest Puerto Rico...the benefits of such immunities... would, of course, be a serious obstacle to the maintenance there of an efficient government."[19] This repeated condescension and outright racism was a key component of the overall strategy to dominate the political future of Puerto Rico, an attitude that continues today, albeit in more toned-down ways.[20] It included an overhaul of Puerto Rico's education system, where Spanish was prohibited from being taught, English became the dominant language of instruction, and U.S. cultural values were imposed in the classroom.[21]

Throughout this period, resistance to the colonial arrangement was growing, led by Puerto Rico's Union Party, which for years had been calling for a resolution to the problem of their lack of fundamental, democratic rights. Policymakers in Washington were clearly not interested in moving quickly on the matter, despite continuous pressure from the island. The option of granting Puerto Ricans U.S. citizenship as a way to guarantee a permanent connection with the United States was discussed repeatedly in Congress, despite the rejection of that option by the island's most visible leaders. From Washington's standpoint, granting islanders citizenship was an easy way to consolidate the relationship between the United States and Puerto Rico, and create a dependency that to this day is used to create a major obstacle to any real discussion of independence as an option for the island. Because of some of the apparent advantages Puerto Ricans receive as a result of their U.S. citizenship, including the ability to travel at will in and out of the country, opponents of independence have been able to instill a level of fear among the population that should the island become independent, Puerto Ricans will lose everything.

With the onset of war in Europe, supporters of granting U.S. citizenship to Puerto Ricans found a strong argument for doing so. Therefore it was not surprising that in 1917, President Wilson signed the Jones Act, which made Puerto Ricans on the island U.S. citizens, and established a bicameral legislature in Puerto Rico whose decisions could be vetoed by the President of the United States. No Puerto Ricans were involved in the debate over citizenship. In essence, it was forced upon islanders, one, to quell the growing displeasure with the prolonged colonial situation, and two, to maintain an active population that could now be added to the U.S. war effort that was being prepared for Europe. Once again, a major transformation in the relationship between Puerto Rico and the

United States had military implications, a fact that has resonance today.

Tens of thousands of Puerto Ricans have fought in the U.S. military over the past eighty years, from the two world wars, Korea, and Vietnam, to some of the more recent escapades in Panama, the Persian Gulf, and Kosovo.[22] Before the United States ended mandatory conscription after the Vietnam War, the prevalence of Puerto Ricans in the military led to the term blood tax, which was used to describe the military draft of men on the island who could eventually lose their life in a war defending U.S. interests, but at the same time could not vote for the president that may have been sending them to war. One need only look at the Korean War as an example of how this blood tax manifested itself in the population. In that conflict, Puerto Ricans had about one casualty for every 600 people, while for the rest of the U.S. population it was a ratio of one casualty for every 1,125 inhabitants; one out of every forty-two casualties in the Korean War was a Puerto Rican.[23] Looking at the war in Kuwait, over 20,000 Puerto Ricans were sent to the gulf to defend the self-determination of Kuwait, while these same 20,000 people could not enjoy self-determination back home.[24] This fact has given pro-statehood islanders ammunition in their quest to make Puerto Rico the nation's fifty-first State. Statehooders, or *annexionistas*, constantly argue that Puerto Ricans have paid their dues and thus warrant the respect and dignity of full representation within the political structure of the United States.[25] What they often fail to point out is that for the most part, the involvement of Puerto Ricans in U.S. war efforts around the world was not a choice made available to the Puerto Rican people, did not improve the welfare of most

Puerto Ricans on the island or in the United States, and perhaps most importantly, did not result in an end to the racist stereotypes and xenophobia that continue to characterize the dominant culture's view of Puerto Ricans.

The granting of U.S. citizenship to Puerto Ricans by no means resolved the status issue. In fact after 1917, the debate over the future of Puerto Rico's relationship with the United States intensified, and has since been at the heart of Puerto Rican politics, both for the main political parties on the island and the millions of Puerto Ricans living in the diaspora.[26]

The popular view of the current legal status is that Puerto Rico is a commonwealth of the United States, although constitutionally, this term really has no substance. The Supreme Court has ruled that Puerto Rico is, in fact, a non-incorporated territory. This means that although the island remains a possession of the United States and is subject to U.S. laws, Washington never intended Puerto Rico to become a state of the Union.[27] This arrangement was clearly a major problem for Washington, where the issue was repeatedly swept under the rug or handled with temporary solutions.[28] It also led to the formation of several important movements that attempted to permanently alter this colonial relationship. In the late 1920s and early '30s, two major figures emerged that would have a lasting impact on Puerto Rican history: Pedro Albizu Campos, a leader of the Nationalist Party and Luis Muñoz Marin, who established the Popular Democratic Party (PPD) in 1938. In looking at the resistance of Puerto Ricans over the past 103 years, it is useful to understand the role that these two leaders played in the struggle for the island's self-determination.

Albizu was a Harvard-educated lawyer who spent years studying in the United States, and was even drafted to serve in the armed forces in 1918. While studying in the United States, Albizu became interested in world liberation movements such as the Irish Republican Sinn Fein. He also witnessed the contradictions of U.S. democracy first hand. A Puerto Rican of African descent, Albizu became agitated by the attitudes of Anglo-Saxon supremacy and outright racism he experienced in Cambridge, Massachusetts. It ignited a fire within him that was evident throughout his analysis of the internal condition of Puerto Rico. For Albizu, the struggle for Puerto Rico's independence could not be separated from other liberation and anti-imperialist movements across the Americas and around the world. He felt there should be no compromise with the United States, and that there was an urgent need for the emergence of a Puerto Rican national conscience in order to break the chains of colonialism.[29]

The nationalists under Albizu demanded independence, and did not recognize the right of the United States to control the internal affairs of the island. They used the U.S. Constitution and the Declaration of Independence as justification for their struggle, and at first carried out their campaign through legal, political means. After seeing this approach fail due to the constant demonization of the independence option for Puerto Rico, they waged a campaign of political attacks and violent confrontations against the United States in an effort to overthrow the colonial government. As a result, Albizu was one in a long line of *independentistas* who was targeted by U.S. and colonial authorities over the years. He was convicted of seditious conspiracy and sentenced to over ten years in

U.S. prisons, where he was subjected to various forms of physical and psychological torture.[30] Albizu never denied his role in wanting to overthrow the U.S. government, and remains to this day a symbol of Puerto Rican patriotism and resistance, even among those who do not advocate independence.[31] The eleven members of the FALN, released in 1999 by President Clinton's limited amnesty, were influenced by Albizu, and represent the latest line of Independence activists who were jailed by U.S. authorities because of their refusal to renounce armed insurrection as a legitimate means to correct the colonial problem of Puerto Rico.

Luis Muñoz Marin, on the other hand, avoided the radical politics of Albizu, taking a more moderate approach to challenging the colonial situation of Puerto Rico. His strategy set the stage for the changes in the relationship between the United States and Puerto Rico that for the most part continue to characterize the island's current status. As the Congress avoided the issue of resolving the status question, Muñoz Marin's PPD pressed for a plebiscite that would allow Puerto Ricans to choose between statehood and independence as their final options. In the late 1930s and early '40s, the majority of the PPD favored Independence. However, as it became clearer each day that President Franklin D. Roosevelt nor the Congress were about to let go of their most prized possession in the Caribbean, and as laws were enacted to criminalize independence activities like those waged by the nationalists,[32] Muñoz Marin adopted his strategy that incorporated the status issue with other issues affecting the Puerto Rican people, such as the dire economic and social effects of the Great Depression. He declared his support for a new political status, what is referred to today as Estado Libre Associado (ELA), the Free Associated State. This approach was meant to give the island more political autonomy, yet maintain and even embrace the very close relationship between the United States and Puerto Rico.

In 1952 this status description was approved by a referendum held on the island. The voters also approved a constitution that for the first time in Puerto Rico's history was written by islanders. Marin became the first governor of Puerto Rico elected by Puerto Ricans. Nevertheless, despite claims by Muñoz Marin and his supporters that the status question was finally resolved with ELA, for all intents and purposes, nothing changed: the Congress still had plenary powers over Puerto Rico. Puerto Rico was not a free state because only Congress could regulate its territories.

With some minor alterations, this is where we find ourselves today, over 102 years after U.S. forces landed on Guánica and hoisted the flag on the island for the first time. Puerto Rican politicians lobby Congress almost daily, demanding a resolution to the status question. Over the years a number of referenda/plebiscites have been held, ostensibly to allow the Puerto Rican people to decide the future of the island's status. The two official plebiscites, in 1967 and 1993, resulted in victories for commonwealth status. Other votes have been held, with the status options, as well as the approach to self-determination, defined in different ways. However, almost all of these popular votes have been shaped by the ruling party at the time of the vote, either the pro-ELA PPD, or the pro-statehood New Progressive Party (PNP) leaving one or more of the political groups dissatisfied with the voting process, if not the results. None of the plebiscites held over the years have been binding for the U.S. Congress. In essence, they have been nothing more than popularity contests, expensive and highly-publicized opinion polls where a lot of rhetoric and propaganda is exchanged from all sides in the media and on the streets, but which have amounted to no fundamental change in the political status of Puerto Rico. In the dawn of the new millennium, Puerto Rico remains a U.S. colony.[33]

THE YOUNG BILL OF 1998 AND THE SAME SONG AND DANCE

The most recent attempt to address the status issue in the legislative arena came in 1998, when Congress took up a bill introduced by Alaska Republican Don Young two years earlier. What the Congress recognized for the first time when the House passed the measure in 1998 was that the colonial relationship was no longer viable. At first the Young Bill called for a plebiscite on the island where Puerto Ricans would vote on only two status options: statehood or independence. It did not provide ELA or any other form of "enhanced commonwealth" as an option, angering the PPD leadership and its rank and file. Later on, it was changed to include ELA only as a temporary status that would have to be reviewed every ten years. The thinking behind this was that the only way to end the colonial status of the island was to either admit Puerto Rico as a state of the union, giving its residents full representation in Congress, or to grant the island its independence from the United States. At the time, Governor Pedro Roselló expressed it like this: "After one hundred years we have a special point in history where the people of Puerto Rico will hopefully have the opportunity of defining after this century long period what the final status of Puerto Rico, what the final definition of that transitional period will be. The Congress of the United States is finally looking at Puerto Rico seriously, and trying to fix the problem that has always existed."[34] He was ignoring the fact that Congress was under no obligation to accept the results of any plebiscite held on the island.

Ironically, during the debate over the Young Bill, the pro-statehood forces found strange bedfellows in the Puerto Rican Independence Party, or PIP. The PIP supported the plebiscite legislation, albeit for different reasons than the PNP. Rubén Berríos Martínez, president of the PIP and a member of the Puerto Rican senate at the time, said: "It places the Puerto Rican problems before the U.S. Congress, and we are convinced that as soon as the United States faces the Puerto Rican issue, it will come to the conclusion that independence is the only way out both for the United States and Puerto Rico. But when nothing happens, when inertia prevails, then the colony keeps on by the law of inertia."[35]

The logic of the PIP was and continues to be that the U.S. Congress is not quite ready to admit Puerto Rico as the fifty-first State, even if the Puerto Rican people were to vote in favor of statehood in a plebiscite. If this were to happen, and Congress did approve such a result, Puerto Rico would automatically have two senators and at least seven representatives in the House, making it more politically powerful than more than twenty other states. Add to that the three Puerto Rican members of Congress that represent large Puerto Rican constituencies in New York and Chicago, and you have yourself a very potent legislative voting bloc, mostly Democratic. Therefore, the PIP reasoned that since the current Free Associated State status had already been discounted by the Congress within the framework of the Young legislation, Washington would have no other choice but to grant the island its independence. This position was expressed repeatedly by Rubén Berríos, who gained national attention in 1999 and 2000 for his year-long act of civil disobedience on the beach in Vieques after David Sanes was killed by a U.S. Naval bomb that went astray. Berríos maintained one of the most visible "peace encampments" on the bombing range during the year of anti-navy protests, and was arrested twice for trespassing onto the bombing range. In 1998, before media attention was focused on Vieques, Berríos warned of the long-term consequences of not granting Puerto Rico its independence: "Even if Puerto Rico were to become a state, that wouldn't solve the problem of Puerto Rican colonialism. The struggle for Puerto Rican independence would continue. The United States doesn't want to have such a problem on its hands. It doesn't want a Palestine or a Northern Ireland in the Caribbean, where the people's desire for national identity remains a fundamental characteristic of its history."[36]

Complicating matters during the debate over the Young Bill were the opponents to the plebiscite legislation who said the bill was deliberately stacked in favor of statehood by Governor Roselló and his supporters. They argued that the Young Bill and its companion legislation in the senate, was not about Puerto Rican self-determination, because it did not offer commonwealth, the current status, as a permanent option. In the bill, commonwealth was described as a temporary status that would have to be brought up again in a public referendum every ten years until one of the other two permanent choices were made by the people. The bill established a vote for either statehood or independence as the final, permanent options. It also spelled out the details for a gradual transition process, once the plebiscite was completed and the results were finally accepted. For the PPD, the Young Bill was seen as primarily the work of the pro-statehood governor, Pedro Roselló, and his very powerful friends in Washington. Carlos Vizcarondo, a member of the Popular Democratic Party and a member of the Puerto Rican Congress, expressed the concerns of his party in an interview back in 1998: "We oppose these bills because of the way they have been written. They're keeping off the ballot the majority of the Puerto Rican people who support the current status, since it has been defined in a way that is not consistent with how we see the current status. In essence, the Puerto Rican people who want to maintain some kind of connection with the United States are going to have to vote for statehood, and lose out everything else that has to do with our language, our culture, our national sports teams, etc."[37]

The Puerto Rican leadership in the United States was also divided over the issue. Of the three Puerto Rican members of Congress, only Rep. Jose Serrano, the Democrat from New York, supported the Young Bill. Chicago Democrat Luis Gutierrez was adamantly opposed to the plebiscite legislation, as was New York Congress member Nydia Velasquez, who voiced her opposition during the debate on the House floor in March 1998: "I am an American citizen born and raised on the island of Puerto Rico. I came to the mainland, was elected to Congress, and stand before this body as a full-fledged member of this legislative body… But I am concerned that a process is about to be imposed on the people of Puerto Rico that is anything but democratic."[38]

As has been the case throughout the last fifty years whenever the issue of Puerto Rico's status has come before the Congress, the entire Puerto Rican leadership was once again debating in the theater of U.S. public opinion. For a moment, it appeared that the PNP and the pro-statehood movement had the upper hand, especially after the House approved the measure. Governor Roselló, convinced that the majority of Puerto Ricans would vote in favor of statehood, rejected accusations that the Young Bill was a predetermined piece of legislation:

> I think there's a problem with the logic in those arguments because these same people [calling the Young Bill a statehood bill] are also saying that Congress and the United States would not accept a Puerto Rican state. They say that Congress would oppose a fifty-first state for Puerto Rico. Yet, how is it that a Congress that would be opposed to statehood for Puerto Rico on the other hand is approving a bill that is favorable to statehood? You know those people have to make up their mind. This is either a bill that's for statehood or a bill that's against statehood. It can't be both and in essence when people read the bill itself they will find that it is a bill that provides an opportunity to choose from three different paths. It starts a movement, it is not the definitive decision. [39]

Ultimately, the Young Bill went nowhere. While it was approved in the House by a narrow margin, the Senate never seriously considered it. Once again, the issue of Puerto Rico's status was not seen as a major priority for the U.S. Congress. The political jostling that took place around the Young Bill was perhaps best summed up by my uncle Tony in a conversation I had with him in his home in Moca after the bill died. He described the never-ending status debates in Congress as a game between a dog and his master. In this game, the master displays the bone to his dog, wags it around to get the dog excited, moves it close to his mouth, and then pulls it away just as the dog is about to bite.

Frustrated by the sudden death of the plebiscite legislation in Congress, where he spent considerable political capital making his case, Governor Roselló later that year sponsored what he described as a *plebiscito Criollo*, in other words, a status vote that was to be generated from within Puerto Rico without the blessing of the U.S. Congress. Its purpose was to send a message to Washington and to the U.S. public in general that the island was indeed ready for statehood. As usual, the vote was nonbinding. It also contained several different status options, including the most ironic and eventual winner, none of the above. This option reflected the opinion of those Puerto Ricans who agreed with the *populares* that the Free Associated State model was not being presented properly in the Young Bill nor in the *plebiscito Criollo*. Some called it a protest vote against the governor, who seemed to stop at nothing to make the plebiscite happen. In essence, it showed once again that most people were not quite ready for statehood, especially if it meant giving up what many perceive to be the benefits of the current status. The ridiculous nature of the referendum and its end result turned out to have the opposite effect on the thinking in Congress and in the U.S. media. Rather than demonstrate that Puerto Ricans were more united than ever vis-a-vis the final political status of the island, it painted a convoluted, almost farcical picture of a people not quite ready for self-determination. Of course, this was not the case, but the governor set himself up for such a political embarrassment in his overzealous push for annexation. Editorials in the *New York Times* and *El Nuevo Día*, as well as political commentators on the island, got considerable mileage out of the fact that in the much touted plebiscite, held 100 years after the U.S. invasion of Puerto Rico, the island was far from resolving its political status.[40]

THE INTERNATIONAL COMMUNITY AS AN ARBITER ON STATUS

For years, the issue of Puerto Rico's status has been brought up at the United Nations, but Washington has always wiggled its way out of any serious debate or criticism. In 1953, after shrewd maneuvering on the part of the United States, Puerto Rico became the first colony to be removed from the list of non-self-governing territories, despite the fact that the newly instituted Free Associated State did not truly resolve the issue of Puerto Rican self-determination.

Since the late 1970s, the UN Decolonization Committee, which is charged with the task of supervising the application of the UN Declaration on Decolonization, has taken up the issue of Puerto Rico. Nevertheless, despite hearing hundreds of representatives from the island and the United States repeatedly denounce the colonial status over the years, it had never come up with a resolution backing the argument that Puerto Rico was indeed a colony of the United States. That is, until July 12, 2000, when the Decolonization Committee approved a resolution that reiterates the right to self-determination for Puerto Rico, and urged the General Assembly to take up the issue.

It was the first time that the committee was able to reach a consensus on the issue.[41] The text of the resolution expressed the committee's hope that the United States would carry out a process that would allow Puerto Ricans to exercise their right to self determination and independence. The committee reached its consensus after hearing from dozens of representatives, both from the island and the United States, voicing pro-statehood and pro-independence views. It recognized the advances that were made in recent years in finding a mechanism that would assure the participation of a broad cross section of the Puerto Rican people to resolve the status question, namely "the proposal to convene a sovereign Constitutional Convention" in Puerto Rico, which, according to several organizations, could offer a solution to the "colonial problem."[42]

The idea of a constitutional convention differs considerably from holding a congressionally approved plebiscite, and has been discussed for years by legal scholars in Puerto Rico. The constitutional convention is based on the idea that the status debate has been stuck in a perpetual limbo because neither political party is willing to give in on some basic principles. The constituent assembly would be made up of citizens elected by popular vote based on a formula approved by the Puerto Rican legislature. They would be representative of the various political groups, and would be assigned the task of coming up with a process that would be presented to the U.S. Congress as the mechanism of finally resolving the status question. The convention could be held without the approval of the U.S. Congress. Nevertheless, because there would be a danger of more political deadlock in such an assembly, the three sides would ultimately be forced to forge alliances with one another in order to achieve their most favorable positions through consensus. By recognizing this mechanism as an important step forward, the UN Decolonization Committee was "breathing new life to an approach that had been raised in the past but that was never explored deeper" because of the "many plebiscites that have been held on the island," said Dr. Jose Luis Mendez, a professor in the School of Social Sciences at the University of Puerto Rico, who wrote *Between Limbo and Consensus* in 1997.[43]

The constitutional convention was endorsed at the UN by several representatives of the independence sector, including former PIP lawmaker David Noriega and the co-president of the Hostosiano National Congress, Carlos Pesquerra.[44] This was seen by many observers as an unprecedented united front on the part of the independence movement, for years split bitterly over strategy and political philosophy.

STATUS DEBATE OR POLITICAL DISTRACTION

Critics of the many attempts that have been made to resolve Puerto Rico's status question say that one of the reasons little has changed is that there are far too many questions and issues that have yet to be properly framed, let alone addressed by the various status formulations or discussions. Any constitutional convention, if ever established, would have to struggle with some of these very complex matters. These issues include who will get to vote in a future plebiscite, only Puerto Ricans on the island, or Puerto Ricans in the United States and elsewhere? If Puerto Ricans in the diaspora will be allowed to participate, how will they be defined? Only those born in Puerto Rico who now live outside of the island, or will it include the children of those individuals born on the island, or anybody else with direct blood relations, even second and third generation Puerto Ricans? As one can see, it becomes very complicated (if you go to the National Puerto Rican Day Parade in New York, for example, you'll find many young people who have never set foot on Puerto Rico who feel no less *boricua* than a person who has lived there all her or his life). To further complicate the issue, what about non-Puerto Ricans who now live on the island, including the many Cuban and Dominican immigrants, as well as U.S. business people? Should they have a voice in any future vote that will determine the island's political status?

Another delicate issue that has yet to be adequately addressed in the various status debates is language. Will English become the official language if Puerto Rico were to become a state, or will it maintain Spanish, or some kind of dual arrangement as its official language, something that was passed into Puerto Rican law under Governor Roselló's tenure, but that would be unprecedented in the history of the United States? Clearly, a lot of people in favor of statehood would resist making English the official language on the island, leading to a swing in votes that may ultimately make it impossible for the statehood status to win in an eventual plebiscite. At the same time, many people in Congress who support accepting Puerto Rico as a state oppose making any special language arrangements for the island's almost 4 million people.[45]

There is also the question of Puerto Rico's Olympic participation. Many Puerto Ricans frown upon the notion of losing their national sports teams, a source of pride for generations. Its baseball and basketball teams have been highly competitive on a number of levels in international forums such as the Olympics and the Pan-American Games. If Puerto Rico were eventually annexed as the fifty-first state, would it mean an end to its representation in international sports competitions?

Another major point of contention in any status debate is the citizenship question. If Puerto Ricans were to vote for independence, however unlikely, would Puerto Ricans lose their citizenship to the United States? Or will they retain a dual citizenship unlike that of any other country, where even those born on the island after Independence would automatically become U.S. citizens as well? While there have been attempts to resolve some of these issues over the years, neither in Puerto Rico nor in the United States has there been a resolution to any one of these questions acceptable to all parties.[46]

It is possible to take it a step further and describe these unresolved questions as mere distractions. Many observers of Puerto Rican history and politics argue that by focusing so much attention over the years on the never-ending status debate, Puerto Rican political leaders and members of Congress have avoided adequately addressing the many other very important issues that shape contemporary Puerto Rican society, such as economic development, cultural preservation, and perhaps most importantly, military occupation. This is based on the argument that says the longer Washington can postpone any real action on Puerto Rico's status, the longer it can strengthen and consolidate the very colonial institutions that people advocating self-determination have been trying to change for generations. This fortification of economic, cultural, and military institutions by the colonial power make it that much more difficult for Puerto Ricans to eventually rid the island of the colonial spell that it has been under since Columbus first landed on Borinquen during his second voyage to the New World at the turn of the fifteenth century.

Perhaps the most significant of these issues involves the United States military presence on the island. Throughout the congressional debates over the Young Bill in 1998, very little was said in the media about the presence of the U.S. Armed Forces in Puerto Rico. This despite the fact that according to the United Nation's own guidelines on decolonization, all military activities by an occupying force should cease completely before any true process of self-determination can take place.[47] In the Young Bill, this factor is completely ignored. Indeed, in discussing the independence status, the bill actually says that under such conditions, the United States would maintain its military bases on the island. In other words, the national security interests of the United States will not be sacrificed by any change in the future political status of Puerto Rico.[48] For many Puerto Ricans, the failure to address the role of the U.S. military in Puerto Rico makes all the previous plebiscites and status debates inadequate.

Throughout 1998, during the 100th anniversary commemorations of the U.S. invasion, Puerto Rican peace and justice activists, along with sectors of the independence movement, organized activities to call attention to the detrimental impact the military has had on the island. Groups like the Caribbean Project of the Peace and Justice Coalition, the Committee for the Defense and Development of Vieques, and the Hostosiano National Congress, held meetings, rallies, and other activities calling for an end to the U.S. military presence in Puerto Rico.

"How can we have a plebiscite with the U.S. Navy continuing its activities as if nothing were going on," asked veteran *independentista* Juan Mari Bras, founder of the Puerto Rican Socialist Party.[49] He argued at the time that if Puerto Ricans were truly going to achieve self-determination as spelled out in United Nations Resolution 1514-XV, they must do so without the overwhelming presence of the U.S. military, a presence that has been expanding in recent years. This argument was perhaps expressed best by long time human rights activist Luis Nieves Falcon, an academic and sociologist who was the coordinator of the Free the Puerto Rican Political Prisoners and Prisoners of War campaign. In discussing the possibilities of holding a truly democratic and open plebiscite where the main status options would be decided on by the Puerto Rican people, Nieves Falcon said:

> "Puerto Rico is a country surrounded by American bases, and I don't think anybody can deny the psychological impact that has on behavior, any behavior, including electoral behavior of people that are surrounded by military posts. Are we going to conduct a decolonization exercise

surrounded by the pressure of American militarism in Puerto Rico? There are many who would argue that this is irrelevant, and that the people accept the U.S. military here. But to many Puerto Ricans, this is a very real threat, and would indeed have an impact on any future vote on the status."[50]

Nowhere is this sentiment felt more than in Vieques, the small island about six miles off the eastern coast of mainland Puerto Rico, where a united front has been openly defying the U.S. military and demanding an end to the navy's presence on the island. The UN Decolonization committee also addressed the grievances of Viequenses in its July 2000 session. In the Committee's resolution, they called for an immediate cessation of military activities on Vieques, a return to "the people of Puerto Rico" lands "occupied by the military," a thorough cleanup of the areas, as well as an end to the persecution of the peaceful demonstrators who had carried out civil disobedience acts against the navy during the course of the previous year.[51] It was the first time the committee took such a strong stand on Vieques, perhaps inevitable given the attention the island had gotten in the previous year. Nevertheless, for years the resistance of the people of Vieques had been otherwise ignored by leaders in Washington, as well as by Puerto Rico's colonial authorities. That is, until April 1999.

AN "ACCIDENTAL" DEATH AND A RESURGENT MOVEMENT

It seems as if protest and resistance were always meant to be part of the social fabric on Vieques. In 1514, Taíno chiefs Cacimar and Yaureíbo fought to the death on the

island they originally called Bieque. Their valiant strug-
gle proved to be the last of the indigenous resistance in
Puerto Rico to the Spanish crown. In 1874, workers in the
Hacienda de Playa Grande in Vieques rebelled against the
repressive working conditions of the Spanish colonizers.
More than seventy of them were jailed in the Fort Count
Mirasol, currently a museum that sits on a Vieques hill-
top overlooking the Caribbean Sea. In 1941, as the U.S.
Navy took over seventy-two percent of the territory of
Vieques, dozens of residents refused to accept the ulti-
matum to leave given to them by the U.S. commanders,
and were forcibly removed only after the bulldozers came
in to take down their homes.

In 1979, fishermen and their supporters blocked naval
maneuvers in an ecumenical protest against the environmental damage and the fishing restrictions placed on
them by the navy. Twenty-one protesters were arrested,
and twelve were sentenced to six months in federal prison,
including thirty-three-year-old Angel Rodriguez Cristobal,
who was later found dead under mysterious circumstances
at the Tallahassee Federal Institution. Angel Ortiz, a member of the Philadelphia Vieques Support Committee, read
this statement at a Philadelphia press conference the day
after Rodriguez was killed while in custody:

> "At approximately 12:06 a.m., on November
> 11th, 1979, Angel Rodriguez Cristobal, a 33-year-
> old inmate at the Tallahassee Federal Institution,
> was discovered in a single cell hanging from a
> sheet rope attached to the front bars of his cell."
> This was part of the press release put out by
> prison officials on the death of Angel R. Cristo-
> bal, Puerto Rican, one of the 21 activists sen-

tenced by Judge Toruella to a six-month prison
sentence for the crime of trespassing on a beach
on the island of Vieques. Angel was killed in Tallahassee, for the crime of stepping on a public
beach in Puerto Rico."[52]

Angel Rodriguez had refused to put up any kind of legal
defense during his sentencing. Like many other Puerto
Rican patriots, Rodriguez declared himself a prisoner of
war, stating that he was involved in a military confronta-
tion with the U.S. Navy, and that he could not be tried in
a federal courthouse, but in front of a military tribunal.
And like the many nationalists before him, he did not recognize the authority of the U.S. federal court in Puerto
Rico. While his death in prison was called a suicide by U.S.
authorities, his friends and family claim there was no rea-
son for Rodriguez to take his own life, and suggest there
was a cover-up around the actual cause of death. In essence,
Rodriguez paid the ultimate price for his protests against
the navy. In response to Rodriguez's mysterious death, two
navy men riding on a bus from the Sabana Seca facility
were killed in an alleged reprisal action, an event
described by *ABC News* correspondent Bill Greenwood as
"confrontations between Navy officials and terrorists."[53]
For years it was the last we would hear about Vieques.

In April 1989, navy officials and federal marshals
clashed once again with peaceful protesters, as they tried
to evict Vieques resident Carmelo Felix Matta from land
that was controlled by the navy. Viequenses responded by
burning two navy vehicles. Later that year hundreds of
families invaded about 800 acres of this navy-held area,
only to be removed by the force of Hurricane Hugo in September of that year.

Then on May 4, 2000, after more than one year of peaceful civil disobedience protests on the U.S. Naval bombing range in Vieques, federal marshals and FBI agents removed thirteen peace encampments and arrested 224 people in what some people called the second invasion of Puerto Rico.[54] The protesters ranged from the president of the Puerto Rican Independence Party, Rubén Berríos Martínez, to Vieques fishermen, from U.S.-based legislators and solidarity activists to church and civic leaders from Vieques and mainland Puerto Rico. Many of them had camped out on the bombing range for months to prevent the U.S. Navy from continuing to use the island as a center for its war games, demanding that not one more bomb be dropped. Although the early morning government sweep allowed the navy to resume its bombing tests by late June, it by no means silenced the protesters. Indeed, it sparked a new wave of resistance actions that led to the arrests of many more prominent political and religious leaders and other activists who refused to accept conditions placed on Viequenses by President Clinton and Governor Rosselló.

The latest round of resistance in Vieques actually began after thirty-five-year-old Vieques resident David Sanes Rodriquez, a civilian security guard on the naval base, was killed on April 19, 1999, by what has been described by the Pentagon as an errant 500-pound bomb dropped by navy planes that missed its target on the Navy's practice range. His death sparked massive protests not only in Vieques, but throughout Puerto Rico and in the United States, and rekindled the resistance to foreign occupiers that has been part of its history since the sixteenth century.

The anger and frustration of Viequenses runs deep, and cuts through the traditional party lines that make up the complex landscape that has characterized Puerto Rican politics for the past century. The navy has controlled more than two-thirds of Vieques since 1941, when it expropriated 26 of the island's 33,000 acres. The takeover of Vieques was part of the U.S. Navy's strategy to occupy the entire Caribbean region as a means of defense against the Germans during World War II, an occupation that spread from Key West in Florida, through Guantánamo in Cuba, Haiti, the Dominican Republic, the Virgin Islands, Puerto Rico, and Trinidad, with Panama as the central point of concern for U.S. forces to defend.[55] Yet Vieques was not the first place where the U.S. military began to take over territory on Puerto Rico. The first major U.S. military base in the region was located in San Juan in the early part of the twentieth century. As far back as 1902, the small island of Culebra housed Camp Roosevelt, which later became a full naval station designed for landing aircraft. As Humberto Garcia Muniz points out in his essay on the military in Puerto Rico in the book *Colonial Dilemma*, Culebra was actually "the first uprooting by U.S. military services of a Caribbean community," as some of its residents were forced to relocate to another area.[56]

Among the most important installations constructed during World War II was the Roosevelt Roads Naval Station in La Ceiba, on the eastern end of Puerto Rico. Roosevelt Roads was originally built to house the entire British navy in case the Nazis invaded Great Britain at the time, and today is the largest U.S. military base outside the continental United States.[57] "Rosy Roads," as U.S.

military officials affectionately call it, led to even further displacement of local communities, perhaps the greatest number being on Vieques, which was to serve as a satellite facility for the base. The actions carried out by the navy to remove Vieques residents are remembered vividly by many of the island's older residents.

During one of my visits in March 1998, about one year before David Sanes' death, I attended a town hall meeting at the Fort Count Mirasol Museum, named after the 1845 colonial governor of Puerto Rico. In the high-ceilinged circular parlor of this nineteenth-century structure, about 100 local residents—fishermen, students, clergy, and community activists—came together to speak out against the constant military maneuvers being conducted by the U.S. Navy on their island. One of the most memorable presentations was given by seventy-four-year-old Lucia Carambot, who talked about what she experienced when the navy arrived back in 1941:

> I can tell you that I may have a number of years on me, but I remember the expropriation as if it were yesterday, because I lived it. We suffered a lot and we continue to suffer up to now. They took people out of their homes and told them that they had to leave within 15 days, or else they would come back with bulldozers and tear down our homes. They threatened us with having to sleep on the street if we didn't accept. And they even took out a woman who was pregnant and about to give birth and told her she had to leave.[58]

Later, during an interview, Carambot described to me how her father refused to leave, and resisted for several years before finally having to give in to the navy. "For us, it's been about 58 years of being surrounded. I say surrounded because to the east and to the west there are military bases. We carry with us an agony and a suffering, because where are we supposed to go? We have nowhere to go. We're trapped," she said in a sharp yet saddened voice that reminded me of my maternal grandmother, who died back in 1972.

Carambot was not the only one to discuss these experiences. In fact, a number of residents shared letters that were sent to them by the Navy that served as orders to vacate. Ramon Rodriguez said he saved his letter in order to remind his children about the way they were treated by the Navy. The letter, dated June 3, 1943, with a heading that said "Officer in Charge of Construction, Naval Air Station, San Juan, Puerto Rico," read:

Vieques, Puerto Rico

The house and land which you occupy in the Municipality of Vieques was acquired by the United States under judgement (sic) of the Federal Court which granted the right of immediate possession.

You will be required to vacate this property within ten days from the date of this notice.

Should you wish to move to another site on Federal Property you will be assigned a suitable area by the Officer-in-Charge of the project upon execution by you of an agreement setting forth the terms upon which your occupancy of the site is permitted.

Yours very truly,
For J.C. Gebhard
Captain (CEC) U.S.N.

Form VB (English)[59]

In 1947 the relocation of the entire population of Vieques to St. Croix was actually discussed by U.S. military planners and colonial authorities, although eventually it was disregarded.[60] Then in the early 1960s, in response to the Cuban revolution, the Kennedy administration began to rethink this idea, proposing to governor Luis Muñoz Marin that all of its residents, as well as the almost 600 residents of nearby Culebra, be relocated. Marin rejected the idea as being "profoundly destructive."[61] In 1975, after intense pressure from people on Culebra, the U.S. Navy finally abandoned the island, making the Vieques facility that much more important for the Pentagon.

Vieques is now divided into three areas. On the west end, the navy maintains a vast munitions storage facility, where hundreds of tons of explosives are stored in over 100 magazines built on hillsides. The navy began conducting an environmental baseline study of this part of the island in June 2000 in order to get it ready for eventual transfer, at least partially, to the Puerto Rican government. This transfer to civilian authorities was put on hold by Congress, however, because some influential members, including Senator James Inhofe (R-OK), felt it would be an incentive for Vieques residents to push even further for the eventual complete withdrawal of the navy from the entire island.[62] These discussions in Congress were proof once again of the way in which Puerto Rican affairs are run entirely by people who have absolutely nothing to do with

Puerto Rico. Ultimately, the land was not to be returned to the people of Vieques anyway, and not even to the government of Puerto Rico, but the U.S. Department of the Interior. In any event, the west end of Vieques is said to be rich in archaeological sites that have not been explored more extensively due to the navy's presence.

On the east end, the navy conducts regular bombing tests from ships, jets, helicopters, tanks, bazookas, and mortars, and experiments with new weapon systems. It should be pointed out that the site is used both by the United States and NATO, as well as by Latin American and Caribbean military forces. In fact, during the recent wave of protests, a controversy emerged when it was discovered on the navy's own website that the navy was renting out a part of the firing range to governments that wanted to test new weapons systems. In January 2001, during the inauguration of the new governor, Sila Maria Calderón, Venezuelan president Hugo Chavez said his military would no longer participate in exercises on Vieques.

Between these two major areas, on a narrow sliver in the middle of the island, lives the civilian population, surrounded by what has become a major component of the Navy's Atlantic Fleet. The navy recognizes Vieques and Roosevelt Roads as the most important military installation in the Western hemisphere. It is here where extensive bombing tests, amphibious landings, and other war games are conducted almost year round, and where many of the navy's global missions are launched, whether to other parts of the Caribbean and Latin America, or to the Middle East and Kosovo. "This is the premier range on the Atlantic fleet where they can bring all their warfare areas together," said Lieutenant Mike Amis, the Atlantic

Fleet's innerrange officer, who coordinated the bombing tests and training maneuvers in Vieques until 1998. "This is the only place that they can do an amphibious landing, giving naval surface-to-fire support, where they can put that all together."[63]

The question most Viequenses have been asking, even before David Sanes was killed by the "errant bomb," is why not conduct these exercises elsewhere? Their concerns include the conventional war games that have been carried out on the island since the mid-1940s, as well as some of the Pentagon's other practices that have had detrimental effects on the island's inhabitants and its ecosystem. They point to several environmental impact studies conducted on Vieques over the last twenty years which demonstrate that the naval maneuvers have created an environmental disaster area of unimaginable proportions, affecting the marine life, fisheries, and vegetation. One individual who has carried out extensive studies on Vieques is environmental scientist Dr. Neftali Garcia, the president of Scientific and Technical Services, an environmental research group based in San Juan. He described how exploded munitions "damaged various lagoons on the eastern end of the island," and created craters that basically make the land in the area useless for any other activity. His reports cite aerial photos that show the navy "had closed connections of the lagoons to the sea, therefore, during dry spells, there was an increase in salinity," leading to the death of thousands of fish in an area once abundant for Vieques fishermen. According to Dr. Garcia, the Navy-built infrastructure and the ongoing bombing tests conducted almost year-round, every year since the 1940s "have increased erosion that has affected other lagoons on the eastern end of the island. There are remnants of metals and explosives in those lagoons, and sediments that have affected aquatic life in those areas. Also, explosions take place in the sea and affect the sea, devastating the fish and therefore ruining the livelihood of those who fish."[64]

This explains the militant role that the fishermen on the island have played in opposition to the navy. For years their voices have been at the forefront of the call to stop the bombing and get the navy out once and for all, led by anti-militarist activist and fisherman Carlos Zenon of the Vieques Fishing Association (VFA). Carlos's two sons, Pedro and Cacimar, were among the resisters who remained hidden in the bombing range after federal marshals removed the peace encampments on May 4, 2000, in essence, continuing the struggle of their father's generation against the navy by risking their lives amidst the dangers of imminent bombing tests. The Vieques Fishing Association represents hundreds of fisherman who at one time flourished in their trade, only to be limited over the years by naval war games. Carlos Ventura, a member of the VFA and a spokesperson for the Committee for the Rights of the Fishermen in Vieques, described it to me as "the worst nightmare that you can have." In a recent interview, he reflected on what the navy's presence has meant to him as a fisherman:

> Since the navy arrived and up to this day, we've had problems with them regarding restrictions on where we can fish. And on top of that, we've had to cope with the destruction of the fish life. Vieques is a place that has abundant fish. It's a place where the Caribbean Sea joins with the

Atlantic Ocean, creating a strong current that in turn gives life to the plankton, which is the basis of the food cycle. Vieques used to be the largest producer of fish and other seafood for all of Puerto Rico. But since then, things have gotten to a point where the fisherman in Vieques is almost nearing extinction. And this is directly related to the bombing practice that takes place regularly on the eastern end of the island.[65]

The navy is said to have "conservation zones" on Vieques that are meant to protect the marine life off its shores. At the Roosevelt Roads Naval Station, visitors can take guided tours of these sites, as if visiting Disney World or Busch Gardens. Winston Martinez, coordinator of the navy's Cultural and Natural Resources Protection Program at the Roosevelt Roads base, said the program was established as a way to deflect some of the criticism that has been directed at the navy for years by local residents, including fishermen like Carlos Ventura. Martinez downplayed the criticism, saying the navy was actually helping the fishing industry in Vieques: "There is no impact on the fish. In fact, when there are maneuvers, fishing is restricted because of the safety of the area. In that way, actually, the maneuvers are helping to conserve the fishing in the area. Because it's not being over-fished, because the area is closed for fishing for two or three weeks at a time."[66]

The concerns Viequenses have about the navy go beyond the fishing docks in the southern part of the island. To a certain extent, what has caused most alarm among the residents of the civilian sector of Vieques is how these war games are affecting the health of the population.

Vieques native Dr. Rafael Rivera Castaño, a retired epidemiologist who taught for years at the University of Puerto Rico School of Public Health in San Juan, led a team of physicians that sounded the alarm about the health risks caused by the navy bombs. They pressured the Puerto Rican Health Department to conduct a study in 1997 to see why the cancer rate in Vieques appeared to be so high compared to mainland Puerto Rico. The study showed that while the cancer rate in Vieques in the 1960s and '70s was lower than it was in the rest of Puerto Rico, by the late '80s, it was 27 percent higher. Released in May 1998, the study was issued by the Central Cancer Registry in Puerto Rico, and showed that while the cancer mortality rate on the main island was 120.4 per 100,000, in Vieques it was 208 per 100,000. Rivera says another study conducted by his colleagues at the School of Public Health showed even more alarming figures: "They did a projection of what's happening in the 90s. That projection states that by 1994 the cancer rate in Vieques was 52% higher than in the rest of the island... What is happening in Vieques? Vieques doesn't have any pharmaceutical industries, no industries that will contaminate the environment. They only have one industry, General Electric that makes switches for electrical switches and that doesn't contaminate. The only thing we can think of that contaminates the environment that would cause this cancer is the Navy."[67]

The apparent negligence of the military was made most evident when it became known that depleted uranium (DU) had been fired on Vieques. One of the most vocal critics of this action was Dr. Doug Rokke, the former director of the Pentagon's Depleted Uranium Project, who denounced the use of depleted uranium on Vieques, a charge the Navy acknowledged. Dr. Rokke, a professor of environmental engineering and science at Jacksonville State University in Alabama, was one of the authors of the Pentagon's program for environmental remediation of formerly used defense sites. Along with criticizing the use of Vieques as a testing ground for conventional munitions, he called the navy "irresponsible if not criminally negligent" for having fired depleted uranium munitions in the area as well.[68] Navy officials acknowledged that they willfully violated "the requirements of the Navy's radioactive materials on firing DU munitions which specify that depleted uranium ammunition is to be used strictly during combat or approved tests and are prohibited from peacetime or training use."[69] Like the bombing that killed David Sanes about two months later, the navy called it an accident. According to a letter written by Luis Reyes, administrator of the Nuclear Regulatory Commission's Region II Office in Atlanta, to Puerto Rico Commonwealth's health secretary, Carmen Melecio dated February 1, 2000, navy officers in Vieques failed to "follow written procedures for issuance and use of ammunition."

Despite violating these strict Pentagon regulations prohibiting the use of DU in non-battlefield conditions, the navy claims the DU is not hazardous to the health of local residents on Vieques. The NRC angered environmental activists when they announced on June 6, 2000, that cleanup plans could leave buried some of the 263 radioactive depleted uranium rounds fired on the Vieques bombing range from the two Marine Corps Harrier jets on February 19, 1999. "The risk of leaving a few buried in the ground is minimal," said the NRC's Reyes. "It should not cause problems in the bombing range because it is an area restricted to the public."[70] This may be the case, only because the area is restricted. But that the buried DU remnants pose no health risks in the short and long term has been written off as pure folly. In January 2001 the United Nations announced that it had found evidence of radioactivity at eight of eleven sites tested in Kosovo that were struck by NATO ammunition with DU. The report was issued in the wake of reports that six Italian soldiers who served in the former Yugoslavia had developed leukemia and died after exposure to spent ammunition.[71]

Dr. Rokke, who was treated in May 2000 for health problems he believes are related to his work studying DU usage in the Gulf War and Yugoslavia, said he believes the navy must "provide complete environmental remediation of all affected terrain and medical care be provided for all affected residents of Vieques."[72] Rokke discounts the navy's claim that there is no health risk to island residents.

Depleted uranium or uranium-238 is made from uranium hexafluoride, which is the nonfissionable by-product of the uranium enrichment process used to obtain uranium-235 for reactor fuel and nuclear bombs. A surprising announcement by U.S. Department of Energy officials on January 29, 2000, acknowledged, after many years of denial, that employees of their facilities had significantly higher incident rates for leukemia, Hodgkin's lymphoma, and cancers of the prostrate, kidney, liver, salivary glands, and lungs. Previous announcements acknowledged respiratory problems at the Paducah, Kentucky facility.[73] Rokke said these revelations and acknowledgments reinforce the suspected health and environmental hazards of depleted uranium, which is manufactured from the main by-product, uranium hexafluoride, of each of these facilities. Rokke added, "It is even more disturbing that in a memorandum dated October 30, 1943, senior scientists assigned to the Manhattan Project suggested that uranium could be used as an air and terrain contaminant. According to the letter sent by the subcommittee of the S-1 Executive Committee on the Use of Radioactive Materials as a Military Weapon to General Groves (October 30, 1943), inhalation of uranium would result in "bronchial irritation coming on in a few hours to a few days." This is exactly what happened to individuals who inhaled DU dust during Operation Desert Storm.[74]

After almost sixty years of this kind of negligence, hundreds of Vieques residents, along with dozens of environmental groups, peace and justice organizations and other activists, began hitting the navy with lawsuits relating to their health concerns and the environmental degradation of the island. Robert Kennedy Jr. was among several high profile lawyers who visited Vieques in June 2000 to investigate the situation on Vieques, only to be denied access to the bombing range by the navy.[75] The navy, meanwhile, continues denying any connection to the illnesses of residents with the Navy's actions. As pressure mounted in the wake of the Sanes and DU accidents, they said they were consulting with the Center for Disease Control's Agency for Toxic Substances and Disease Registry regarding the claims, noting that "no scientific study based on empirical data has ever linked Navy activities on Vieques to any civilian health issues."[76]

The April 19, 1999, death of David Sanes was the end of the line for the people of Vieques. Sanes's death galva-

nized the entire community, and brought together sectors
from the many different political tendencies of Puerto
Rico for the first time with the sole purpose of resisting
the navy. The peace encampments began almost immediately, a militant act of defiance by people who were often
described in the media as trespassers, but who saw themselves carrying out their duty to protect civilian lives and
the environment of this small island. It forced the Navy's
Atlantic Fleet to suspend maneuvers, specifically two of
its crown jewels, the USS George Washington and the USS
Eisenhower, which had to turn away from Vieques and
carry out its war games elsewhere.

This unprecedented coalition of political and social
forces from Vieques, mainland Puerto Rico, and the United
States held together for months. And they most likely
would have prevailed in getting the Navy out sooner had
former Governor Roselló not agreed to an executive order
issued by President Clinton in early January. In fact, the
May 4 crackdown and arrests were presented to the U.S.
public as a necessary measure to deal with "the intransi-
gent protesters" who refused to accept the agreement
between Roselló and Clinton.[77] The so-called agreement
was not discussed beforehand with Vieques residents.

In carrying it out, Roselló ignored the overwhelming
opposition throughout the island against the navy. The
agreement allowed for bombing tests to resume, albeit
without live ammunition. It also limited the military
maneuvers to ninety days of the year, considered by the
navy to be a major concession. Another controversial
aspect of the agreement was the proposed referendum to
be held on Vieques "to allow residents to vote" on
whether or not they want the navy to leave within three

years, or remain on the island, as if the protests and outrage were not enough evidence that the navy was no longer welcome. It earmarked a $40 million development package for the island, with an additional $50 million thrown in should Viequenses vote in favor of letting the navy stay put.

To Governor Roselló, President Clinton, and to a lesser extent, the navy, this agreement appeared good enough to calm things down after over a year of tension. But the people of Vieques were serious when they made their rallying cry, "Ni una bomba mas" ("Not one more bomb"). Washington-based attorney Falvio Cumpiano, who represents the Committee for the Rescue and Development of Vieques, said it best when he stated "the people of Vieques will not be bought off by $40 million, and will not participate in a vote that does not include as one of the options that the navy leave immediately."[78]

So the resistance continued and even strengthened. After the initial arrests in May, protesters continued entering the bombing range on several occasions to continue the civil disobedience campaign against the navy, including in June, when the navy resumed its bombing runs despite overwhelming opposition. These actions were spearheaded by members of the Puerto Rican Independence Party, and its leader, Rubén Berríos Martínez. Hundreds of PIP activists were rounded up as a result of these protests, reminding islanders once again of the repression against the Independence movement that has occurred throughout the past one hundred-plus years. It was therefore quite an outrage for PIP leaders and their supporters to hear former governor Carlos Romero Barcelo, Puerto Rico's resident commissioner in Washington at the time, say was Berríos was one of several outsiders manipulating Viequenses about how to think, outsiders made up mainly by the pro-independence sector of Puerto Rican politics.[79]

Contrary to what people like Roselló, Romero Barcelo and U.S. senator James Inhofe say about the ongoing protests, the opposition to the navy is by no means isolated or limited to some outsiders or troublemakers. Many sectors of Puerto Rican society joined the call for the immediate withdrawal of the navy and an end to all bombing, including leading figures in the church, well-known intellectuals, artists, celebrities, the Puerto Rican members of Congress, and other elected officials. The death of David Sanes united Puerto Ricans like no other event in the last fifty years, for the first time directly challenging Washington. The arrogance of the navy and its supporters was to the people of Vieques a stark reminder of the colonial relationship that has existed for over 102 years, a relationship that considers Puerto Rican interests second to U.S. interests. Governor Roselló, in accepting the Clinton proposal, was in the eyes of Viequenses, no different than the colonial puppets installed by Washington in the wake of General Miles's invasion in 1898. For Vieques and for the people of Puerto Rico, it has never been clearer: this colonial relationship must be terminated.

The universal opposition of Puerto Ricans to the navy in Vieques was made very clear on June 11, 2000. The National Puerto Rican Day Parade in New York, the largest annual gathering of Latinos in the United States, was dedicated to the struggle of the people of Vieques, as well as to the memory of the father of Puerto Rican nationalism, Don Pedro Albizu Campos. Some leaders of the PNP and the PPD boycotted the parade because of the dedication's implied connection between Vieques, which all Puerto Ricans support, and the most controversial figure of the independence movement. Others considered the dual dedication appropriate, considering that Don Pedro was one of the first leaders to speak out against the navy in Vieques back in 1940.

Regardless, the parade was filled with signs, banners, and chants against the navy. People along the parade route cheered as Vieques activists, fishermen, women, and children marched with their fists raised in the air. Some would write it off as nothing but a symbolic gesture that ultimately did not stop President Clinton from resuming bombing tests in Vieques just a few weeks later. Yet there is no doubt that the event was special. It was a massive protest mobilization at an event traditionally known for its mainstream politics and excessive commercialism. For one steamy June Sunday afternoon in New York City, over one million Puerto Ricans lined the streets of New York's Fifth Avenue demanding: "Fuera Marina de Vieques! U.S. Navy Out of Vieques!"

Cacimar and Yaureíbo, the two Taíno chiefs who resisted the Spanish to the death on Vieques in the sixteenth century, would have been proud!

Less symbolic and more concrete were the results of the November 7, 2000, elections for governor. The hotly contested race between Carlos Pesquerra, the candidate of the pro-statehood PNP, and Sila Maria Calderón of the PPD, hinged greatly on the issue of Vieques. Calderón won by a little more than four percentage points, becoming the first woman to be elected governor of the island. During the campaign, Calderón had pledged to pull out the spe-

cial operations units of the police away from the area of
Camp Garcia where civil disobedience against the navy
continued; committed herself to dedicating more funds
to conduct extensive epidemiological tests on the island;
and criticized the date and the nature of the proposed referendum, one, for being scheduled too late in the year, and
two, for not offering as one of the options to voters that
the navy leave Vieques right away.[80] She basically took
the position that the navy needed to get out of Vieques
as soon as possible. Political analysts attributed her vic-
tory to the strong stance she took on Vieques, as well as
to the about face taken by Governor Roselló earlier in the
year when he accepted Clinton's January 2000 Executive
Order, something that did not bode well for the PNP candidate in the general elections.[81]

PUERTO RICO AND THE POST-COLD WAR U.S. MILITARY STRATEGY

While the Pentagon says Vieques and the other military
installations in Puerto Rico are essential to defend the
national security of the United States, protesters continue
to argue that this is false. They point to the fact that the
navy went a whole year during the peace encampment
protests from April 1999 to May 2000 without using the
island for heavy-weapons bombing tests or other strategic maneuvers. If it is possible to go a year without tests,
why not find another site altogether?

So what role does Vieques and Puerto Rico play in
overall U.S. strategy in the region? For starters, with the
implementation of the Carter-Torrijos Treaty, which
stipulated a U.S. withdrawal from Panama and the
relinquishment of the Panama Canal to Panamanian
authorities, the United States Southern Command

(USSOUTHCOM) was forced to leave Panama. As a result, Puerto Rico became the new home of the U.S. Army South (USARSO) and Special Operations Command (SOCSOUTH), a sub-unified, joint-service command of USSOUTHCOM. The joint commands are housed in the principal U.S. bases in Puerto Rico, including Fort Buchanan, Fort Allen, and Roosevelt Roads, with some of the training operations conducted at Camp Santiago, operated by the Puerto Rican Army National Guard.[82] Although SOUTHCOM headquarters moved from Panama to Miami, many of the military operations are carried out by planners in Puerto Rico, making the island "the biggest player in the region," according to retired army general Felix Santoni, deputy commander-in-chief for mobilization and reserves at SOUTHCOM in the early 1990s.[83]

Many of the SOCSOUTH operations conducted within Roosevelt Roads are considered top secret, but are known to include Green Berets, Navy Seals, and Marine infantry units that carry out all the special tasks under SOUTHCOM. Their mandate includes "anti-drug" and "anti-terrorist" operations, training of regional military forces, and so-called humanitarian missions, such as emergency relief.

Officially, the function of SOCSOUTH in Puerto Rico is to serve as intelligence and logistical support for the 500-member U.S. teams in the counter-drug installations in the Dutch-held islands of Curacao and Aruba, as well as the controversial U.S.-built "counter-narcotics" airfield in La Manta in northwestern Ecuador, just south of the Colombian border. These are the so-called Forward Operating Locations, also known as FOLs, which are to be used to support aerial counter-drug missions in the

Central American and Andean region. In November 1999, the United States and Ecuador signed a ten-year agreement for the use of La Manta airfield for interagency counter-drug flights, drawing considerable opposition from within Ecuador by people concerned with a growing U.S. military role in their country, and the dangers of getting Ecuador tied into the internal conflict in Colombia.[84]

In March 2000, the United States signed a similar ten-year agreement with the Netherlands for the FOL on the islands of Aruba and Curacao, and a ten-year agreement with El Salvador for the use of Comalapa Air Base,[85] also with considerable opposition from anti-interventionist forces in El Salvador. These arrangements demonstrate that, with Panama no longer in the picture, Puerto Rico has become the essential coordination and communications component of this regional military infrastructure.

For example, the Southern Command operates at least seventeen radar systems ostensibly to track presumed drug flights. Three are in Peru, another four are in Colombia, and the remaining are undisclosed and come under the Air Force's Caribbean Basin Radar Network. Add to these installations the navy's much-touted Relocatable Over the Horizon Radar, or ROTHR, one located in the south-central town of Juana Díaz and the other in Vieques, and you have a complex radar network said to be able to detect aircraft in cocaine-producing jungles in the Amazon basin, and give fighter jets enough raw intelligence to intercept them.[86] So despite the end of the Cold War, Puerto Rico's importance to the United States as a military center has not diminished at all.

"The drug war has become the justification of the U.S. to maintain this military presence, all the while blurring the lines between civilian and military functions in law enforcement," said Dr. Jorge Rodriguez Beruf, a professor of political science at the University of Puerto Rico.

He and other critics of the military argue that the United States strategy has shifted only in its stated purpose from combating the Cold War to combating the drug war. In the end, the result is the same: U.S. military forces maintaining a firm grip on the region to make the hemisphere safe for Washington's interests, very often involving direct intervention, as appears to be the case in the U.S.'s growing role in Colombia's internal war.

And because nothing has fundamentally changed, in Puerto Rico, peace and justice activists are continuing to mobilize in the wake of the death of David Sanes. While their primary demand is to get the navy out of Vieques, they hope to call attention to the negative impact the military has had, not only on Vieques, but throughout all of Puerto Rico.

PUERTO RICO IN THE MEDIA: COLONIALISM DOES NOT EXIST

It can be argued that one of the tools of maintaining a colonial system in place is the deliberate manipulation of the media in order to keep the colonial subjects misinformed. Perhaps more effective, however, is making sure the people whose interests are supposedly being served by maintaining a colonial regime in place in a certain part of the world, are kept in the dark about what is going on "back in the colonies." To a certain extent, if we observe U.S. media coverage of Puerto Rico, we can see this latter model operating in full effect. Indeed, throughout the past 100 years, misinformation, lies, and distortions have been part of the regular fare when it comes to coverage of Puerto

Rico, making it understandable why there is a general misunderstanding if not ignorance on the part of the U.S. public regarding the island, its people, and its politics.

From the justification for the Spanish-American War and the subsequent 1898 invasion of the island, to the early rumblings in the Congress about what to do with "Porto Rico," U.S. news reports were characterized by racist language based on the myth of Anglo-American supremacy, as well as distortions of events that were designed to strengthen the hand of U.S. policymakers who had the interests of their constituencies in mind, at the expense of the interests of Puerto Rico.[87]

Looking to the present, there is no question that the Puerto Rico "story" is a complex one, which could be why the U.S. media do not consider it a top priority. As I mentioned at the outset, a number of recent developments forced the media to once again pay attention to Puerto Rico, namely the Vieques situation, as well as the release of the FALN prisoners. The overt racism of the past has diminished. However, what we see in today's coverage is that the tendency to frame events within the perspective of U.S. politics and strategic interests remains unchanged. Indeed, if we look at how the two agenda-setting newspapers of the country, the *New York Times* and the *Washington Post*, covered Puerto Rico between April 1999 and July 2000, we can begin to understand why so many misconceptions remain about the island, both on the part of non-Puerto Rican politicians and the broader public.

The *Times* waited a long time to report on the growing resistance to resumed military training on Vieques. For two months after the protests began, the *Times* failed to go beyond picking up short news service items on what killed David Sanes. On July 10, 1999, the paper finally published a 1,400-word account headlined "Uproar against Navy War Games Unites Puerto Ricans."

"For the first time since its acquisition by the United States after the Spanish-American War, Puerto Rico, a self-governing commonwealth and an American military *outpost* in the Caribbean, is demanding that the Navy end all military activities in Vieques and return the land it acquired in the 1940's [emphasis added]." As we have already seen, this is hardly the first time that Puerto Ricans have petitioned the navy to leave Vieques. Although the article noted (in parentheses), "Similar protests had led the Navy to stop exercises in Culebra in 1975," it avoided saying that Vieques was then forced to pick up Culebra's burden. Meanwhile, by calling the island "self-governing," the link between Puerto Rico's political status and Vieques protests was conveniently ignored.

Eventually, the *Times* reported the only story that viewed Vieques through the lens of Puerto Rico's unequal relationship with the US: "Puerto Ricans Gain Ear of Washington But Seek Far More" (Dec. 5, 1999). The article primarily relied on the testimony of Rubén Berríos Martinez, head of the PIP, which the writer called a "miniscule movement eclipsed in the four decades since Puerto Rico became a commonwealth of the United States"

The *Times* article described the protests that followed the civilian's death: "For two months now, about three dozen people have occupied the eastern tip of this small island seven miles off Puerto Rico, *trespassing* on property controlled by the United States Navy in an act of deliberate defiance." Because the navy expropriated (the article says "acquired") the land—often with little or no remuneration—who's "trespassing" on whose property is still a matter for debate. The navy's "expropriation" was mentioned in only a few articles on Vieques, and just one told this story: "Many who have joined the protests, such as sisters Severina Guadalupe, 72, and Luisa Guadalupe, 82, had their childhood homes expropriated by the navy and then flattened by its bulldozers... [their] father was paid just $50 for his land" (*Post*, Dec. 9, 1999).

Between April 1999 and July 2000, the *Times* and the *Post* published reports that did very well at explaining the importance of Vieques to the U.S. military and the political implications of the insurrection in Washington and New York, but failed to lay out the history behind the protests themselves.

A *Times* editorial by a former Defense Department employee dated May 2, 2000—as federal agents were making final preparations to clear the range—revealed that department officials "all accepted as inevitable that once the Culebra situation was resolved (in 1975), protests would be likely to begin on Vieques, and the training there would have to go next." After nearly a decade of worsening relations with the Viequenses, the navy agreed to a Memorandum of Understanding with the commonwealth in 1983. The memorandum—which promised to limit bombing, protect wildlife, and improve infrastructure—was rarely referred to, and the navy's failure to honor its promises, even more rarely. "For decades there have been complaints about Navy activity on the island, and in 1983 the Navy signed a memorandum with Puerto Rico promising to change its behavior" (*Times*, Dec. 4, 1999). The terms of the memorandum and the Navy's specific violations of it were not presented in the *Times* or the *Post*, and only once was it reported that the navy itself "concedes that it contributed to the ill will in Puerto Rico by failing to fulfill a 1983 agreement that ended the last round of protests" (*Post*, Oct. 2, 1999).

Although claims that the navy has polluted Vieques were registered in the *Times* and *Post*, concrete evidence of environmental abuse was rare. *Times* articles limited description of the Viequenses grievances to: "The small island has high unemployment; its residents have suffered health problems, including a high incidence of cancer, and the island's coral reef and wildlife have been threatened by the bombing." One *Times* reporter literally repeated this phrase, with minor variation, in four of the eight articles she filed. She elaborated in substance only once, near the end of a short article on pg. A25. (Oct. 20, 1999): "Members of the Presidential panel... criticized the Navy for creating this crisis by failing to address long-held grievances of the people of Vieques. They said the range was largely responsible for an unemployment rate of 25 percent on the island, which might otherwise be a desirable tourist spot, and environmental and health problems." Finally, a number!

A few articles in the *Times* and *Post* noted that significantly more people live in poverty on Vieques than in other parts of Puerto Rico. "But," wrote a *Times* reporter, "Vieques attracts about 4,000 tourists a year, drawn to its pristine beaches, bioluminescent bays and slow pace" (July 10, 1999). The reporter didn't explain that 4,000 tourists annually is significantly fewer than visit other Caribbean islands. It was noted in congressional testimony that the

British Virgin Islands—only a few square miles larger than Vieques—annually receives 1,000 times more visitors; Bermuda—less than half the size of Vieques—has over 4,000 hotel rooms, compared to Vieques' 100. Governor Rosselló recalled before Congress that *The Wall Street Journal* had recently ranked the island one of the world's five worst vacation spots. Some months later, the *Times' Travel Desk* ran a 2672-word story (longer than any news story the paper published on Vieques) that made such patronizing observations as: "Camp Garcia had retarded the island's development, kept it poor, natural, and charming." A February 22, 2000, article in the *Post* about Puerto Rican protests against the plan to phase out military training at Vieques noted: "Sen. Frank H. Murkowski (R-Alaska) said he would introduce a counterproposal that would allow the Navy to keep its bombing range on the eastern end of Vieques since pollution from 60 years of bombing may make the area permanently uninhabitable." This seems to be a statement that needed further examination, not only by the U.S. Senate, but by the media outlet disseminating it, in this case the *Post*.

No *Times* article about the Navy's impact on Vieques reported that the navy illegally dropped napalm on the island in 1993 and denied it repeatedly. During the same time period, the *Post* made only two passing references to napalm use on Vieques—both in one article published on August 19, 1999. The article reported that the Puerto Rican secretary of state "alleged that Navy officials lied to her in public hearings about using napalm." That they lied was more than an allegation—military officials denied they had deployed napalm on Vieques until July 1999. Neither the *Times* nor the *Post* reported the Navy's reversal. The possible effects of napalm contamination were not discussed.

The *Times* and the *Post* repeatedly trumpeted federal officials' claims: "Navy officials say...," "The Defense Department says...," "Some senior military officers worry...," "a White House official said," "The Pentagon insists," etc. The instances of this kind of sourcing are almost too many to describe. The articles weighed heavily on the side of military sources, but rarely questioned any of their assertions. Whether or not these exercises were indeed "vital" was not investigated by the *Post* or the *Times*, whose reporters seemed to limit themselves to asking the opinion of sitting military officials. Only one mention—in a *Post* editorial—was made of a former admiral's statement to the commonwealth's commission on the U.S. military in Vieques, although his most damaging testimony was not quoted. "The Marine Corps doesn't do opposed amphibious landings anymore, hasn't since Inchon in Korea," the admiral said.

None of the articles in either paper mentioned the Armed Service Committee Chairman's directive to the navy—twenty years ago—to seek an alternative site to Vieques. Instead, the *Post* reported: "The Defense Department says that despite months of searching, it has found no replacement for the range" (Oct. 19, 1999). The article failed to explain that there is no replacement because the military long refused an order to find and develop one.

On October 20th, two days after a presidential panel consisting mostly of military men recommended resuming bombing at Vieques, the *Times* ran a 579-word story headlined "Puerto Rico Governor Faces Senators Over Firing Range." The article included three quotes from military sources, and paraphrased one senator's comments: "Senator James M. Inhofe... said the firing range should be reopened immediately." On the other hand, only one remark—and one of the most innocuous—of Gov. Rosselló's was quoted (in the last paragraph). None of the Vieques representatives who testified before Congress that day were quoted, consulted, or even mentioned.

Then on December 4th, the day after Clinton offered "major concessions to Puerto Rican authorities and protesters...(by agreeing) to halt live-fire exercises on the island of Vieques and promised that within five years the Navy will abandon the bombing range," (*Post*) both papers devoted 1000-odd words to the story. Reporters quoted two military officials, a senator, the president, the vice president, Hillary Clinton, and a "senior administration official." Gov. Rosselló and Independence Party President (referred to as a "member" of the party in the *Times*) Berríos Martínez were the sole Puerto Ricans consulted. Both papers reported essentially the same statement by Berríos Martínez: "Now is the time to strengthen our resolve behind... 'Not one more shot.'"

As I mentioned earlier, Puerto Ricans' resolve did strengthen, although Rosselló's did not. Two months later, the *Times* reported: "Puerto Rico agreed today to let the Navy resume limited training on the island of Vieques..." (Feb. 1, 2000). When the first round of negotiations collapsed in December, the *Times* reported that "the governor rejected the Navy's latest proposal." But when the deal went through, all of "Puerto Rico" was suddenly on board. Of course, as the ongoing protests and the November elections illustrate, all of Puerto Rico was not on board with the Clinton Executive Order. Protesters continued to

occupy the range, in defiance of the terms of the deal, until
federal agents "swept" in and removed them, "ending a
protest that had been an irritant to the Clinton administration for nearly a year" (May 5, 2000). Sixty years of
resistance by the people of Vieques was written off by the
Times as a mere "irritant."

While Vieques was reported by these two shining
examples of U.S. journalism primarily within the prism
of U.S. military and strategic interests, President Clinton's offer of clemency to members of the FALN in
August 1999 was overwhelmingly reported within the
framework of U.S. party politics. The emphasis from the
beginning was on Clinton's offer, and the political reper-
cussions—Democrats were divided and Republicans
accused Clinton of using the offer to win Latino votes for
his wife in her New York Senate bid, which escalated into
a direct challenge to the President's right to executive
privilege. That the campaign to free the Puerto Rican
prisoners had broad national and international support
after years of organizing on the part of grassroots
activists was a non-issue in the reports filed by the *Times*
and the *Post*. "Clinton to Commute Radicals' Sentences"
read the *Times*'s headline announcing the offer on August
12, 1999. The 570-word article ran in on page fifteen.
Although the first paragraph reports that the "radicals"
are "members of a Puerto Rican nationalist group that
was involved in more than 100 bombings," not until the
seventh paragraph is it explicitly stated, "those whose
sentences the President wants to commute were not
directly involved in…deaths and injuries." The activities
for which they were convicted are summed up as "crimes
like seditious conspiracy, possession of an unregistered

firearm or interstate transportation of a stolen vehicle." For these nonviolent crimes, "some were sentenced to more than 50 years in jail, a length of time that the President viewed as excessive." More accurately, most of the convicted members (nine of sixteen) offered clemency were sentenced to at least fifty-five years, and some as high as ninety-five years. Whether or not the sentences were excessive was not investigated or discussed in the *Times* or the *Post* throughout the months of debate over the President's offer.

Three days later, the story was demoted to the *Times*'s *Metro* section, and reported for its possible effects on the Senate race. Seven of eighteen *Times*'s hard news articles on the clemency offer were *Metro* stories (e.g., "Giuliani Questions Timing by First Lady on Clemency," "Mrs. Clinton Denies Role in President's Clemency Offer"), as if the struggle for Puerto Rican independence and self-determination was a simple local matter of interest only to New Yorkers. The philosophy and nature of the nationalist's struggle, whether one agrees with their tactics or not, were thereby rendered irrelevant.

The *Post*'s hard news stories were, naturally, all national, and the overwhelming majority (eleven of thirteen) were primarily about the political implications of the commutation ("Lawmakers Weigh in on FALN Clemency," "Senate Assails Clemency Order," "No Letup in Probes of Clinton Presidency," "Clinton Explains Clemency; Politics Had No Role in Decision, President Tells House Member," "Impact on Gore Mentioned in FALN Clemency Memos").

Perhaps not surprisingly, there was no attempt at analyzing Puerto Rican politics or the history of U.S. colonial rule, which might have helped contextualize the FALN's activities and inform the group's extralegal methods of registering protest, methods that have their origins in the U.S. Revolutionary War of the late eighteenth century. Only one article linked the clemency offers to Puerto Rico's political status: "Still roiled by opposition to the presidential clemencies recently granted to Puerto Rican militants, New York politicians of Puerto Rican heritage have asked the Senate to hold public hearings on the ultimate political status of Puerto Rico just as it is holding hearings on the clemencies" (*Post*, Sept. 19, 1999). Obviously, this is a "Puerto Rican" issue.

Furthermore, the group was often described—although generally indirectly (e.g., in quotes by U.S. law enforcement officials)—as a "terrorist" organization, despite the fact that its targets were overwhelmingly military, and not directed primarily against civilians. The members offered clemency were often themselves labeled "terrorists" in the same way, even though none of them were convicted on counts of violent crime. Rarely were the commutations discussed in relation to the protests on Vieques, despite the obvious connection, or the long tradition of resistance to U.S. colonial rule in Puerto Rico. The same September 19th article mentioned above put it this way: "Seizing the moment to put forward another issue that has rumbled, though less explosively than the clemencies, in the prospective Senate campaign of first lady Hillary Rodham Clinton, the 15 legislators also want the Senate to hold hearings on the Navy's use of Vieques Island." Here, the connection is not the commonwealth status of Puerto Rico, but rather Hillary Clinton's senate campaign.

Finally, the papers failed to report the U.S. government's persecution of its own citizens in Puerto Rico,
whereby "subversives" were spied on, harassed, and, in
some cases, murdered, making political protest dangerous
and ineffective, and forcing those advocating independence to seek alternative methods to achieve their goals.

PUERTO RICAN RESISTANCE INTO THE 21ST CENTURY

The Puerto Rican national spirit cannot be broken, regardless of the political limbo in which the island lives. The
colonial arrogance of the United States as well as the ignorance of its political, economic, and media elite, has provided fuel to the resistance of a people who refuse to let
go of the centuries-old dream of true self-determination.
Over 102 years of U.S. colonialism, characterized by political deceit, economic exploitation, social dislocation, cultural domination, and military occupation, have not been
enough to dilute the cultural pride of the Puerto Rican
people. Yes, the people continue to be far from unified in
their feelings regarding the future of the island's status.
Nevertheless, as the navy's bombing in Vieques and the
release of the FALN prisoners have shown, more and more
Puerto Ricans are being forced to see the history of U.S.
control over their island not as a benevolent one, but one
laced with hypocrisy and contradiction.

Those who still believe full annexation is the solution to the island's problems slowly are beginning to
understand that Main Street USA is not quite ready to
accept Puerto Rico as an equal, just as the majority of
Puerto Ricans are not about to sell themselves down the
road of cultural annihilation. I remember a few years back
when former Governor Roselló, in his defense of making

Puerto Rico a state, uttered that Puerto Rico was not a nation, he generated a mass mobilization on the island which was dubbed "La Nacion en Marcha" (a nation on the move). The show of force brought together over 150 thousand people into the streets of San Juan, defiantly telling the colonial government, and indeed the world, that the Puerto Rican nation lives! Their resistance, as well as that of the people of Vieques, and the jailed Puerto Rican Nationalists, expose the shame of the United States of America, the last colonial power of the modern world.

Notes

1. Pedro Roselló, interview by author, La Fortaleza, Old San Juan, Puerto Rico, May 14, 1998.

2. Rubén Berríos Martinez interview by author, Senate office, Puerto Rican Congress, Old San Juan, March 20, 1998.

3. FOR-TFLAC is based in San Francisco, and formerly published a quarterly newsletter, *Panama Update*. They have since shifted their focus to demilitarization, decontamination, and development in Puerto Rico. They can be contacted at forlatam@igc.org.

4. See Tom Barry and John Lindsay-Poland, *Inside Panama: The Essential Guide to Its Politics, Economy, Society and Environment*, (Albuquerque, N.M.; Interhemispheric Resource Center, 1995).

5. The one-hour radio documentary *One Flag, One Territory: Panamanian Sovereignty in the Post-Cold War Era* was broadcast in May 1994 and distributed nationally by Pacifica Radio. It is now available through the Pacifica Radio Archives based in Los Angeles (800-735-6230; www.pacifica.org).

6. *Puerto Rico: Reflections on the Oldest Colony* was originally broadcast on WBAI, 99.5FM, in New York on July 25, 1998, and rebroadcast on Pacifica Radio's *Democracy Now*. It was distributed by Pacifica and aired on over 100 stations nationwide. It is now available through the Pacifica Radio Archives, based in Los Angeles.

7. For a thorough account of the Puerto Rican nationalists jailed for their activities seeking the independence of the island, see Ronald Fernandez, *Prisoners of Colonialism: The Struggle for Justice in Puerto Rico* (Monroe, Me.: Common Courage Press, 1994).

8. Jose E. Serrano, "Dialogue Opens About FBI/Carpetas Questions," *El Nuevo Dia*, March 26, 2000; For a thorough documentation on the repression of Puerto Rico's independence movement, see Ramon Bosque Perez, and Jose Javier Colon Morera, *Las Carpetas: Represion Politica y derechos civiles en Puerto Rico, Ensayos y Documentos*, (Río Piedras, Puerto Rico: Centro para la investigación y Promoción de los Derechos Civiles (CIPDC), 1997).

9. There are numerous books on the early history of indigenous communities in Puerto Rico and their interaction with the Spanish. See Arturo Morales Carrion, *Puerto Rico: A Political and Cultural History* (New York, W.W. Norton, 1983); also Jose Barreiro, *The Indian Chronicles* (Houston: Arte Público Press, University of Houston, 1993).

10. For more detailed study of the Spanish-American War, there are numerous works, including David Trask, *The War with Spain in 1898*, (New York: Macmillan, 1981); also Morales Carrion, *Puerto Rico*, 129-152.

11. Jose Trias Monge, *Puerto Rico: The Trials of the Oldest Colony in the World* (New Haven, Conn.: Yale University Press, 1997), 22.

12. See Juan R., Torruella, *The Supreme Court and Puerto Rico: The Doctrine of Separate and Unequal* (San Juan, Puerto Rico: Editorial Universidad de PR, 1988), 10-17.

13. Throughout the controversy over the navy's use of Vieques as a practice bombing range that resulted in the wake of the death of David Sanes, countless statements were made by U.S. military officials, the White House, and conservative members of Congress echoing this national security concern.

14. Toruella, *Supreme Court*, 15.

15. Ibid., 15-17.

16. Ibid., 19.

17. *"We have not come to make war upon the people of a country that for centuries has been oppressed, but on the contrary, to bring you protection...to promote your prosperity, and to bestow upon you the immunities and blessings of the liberal institutions of our government"*; General Nelson Miles, July 25, 1898, Guánica, Puerto Rico, from the *Annual Reports of the War Department*, Washington, D.C., 1902; reprinted in *Documents on the Constitutional History of Puerto Rico*, 2nd ed., (Washington, D.C.: Government printing office, 1964).

18. Trias Monge, *Puerto Rico*, 1-3.

19. Ibid., 40, citing G.W. Davis, *Report on Civil Affairs in Porto (sic) Rico*, 56th Cong., 1st sess., H.R. 2, 481.

20. See Ronald Fernandez, *Disenchanted Island*, especially chapters 1-4, where numerous examples of this racist attitude are presented; Juan Gonzalez, *Harvest of Empire: A History of Latinos in America* (New York: Vintage Books, 1999), where the author dedicates an entire section to the idea of imperial culture as a means to dominate and indeed justify colonialism.

21. See Ronald Fernandez, *Disenchanted Island* (Stanford, Conn.: Praeger, 1994), 55-59. In this regard, I recall a visit I made to Mayaguez, Puerto Rico, in 1991, when I spent the day with Puerto Rican nationalist and former political prisoner Dr. Rafael Cancel Miranda, one of four *independentistas* who shot up the U.S. Congress in 1954. As we walked through his old neighborhood, he showed me the school from where he said he had been expelled because of his refusal to speak English. The emotions running through his voice at the moment was just one manifestation of his passion and commitment to Puerto Rican independence, something I've admired in the many instances I've seen him since, either during interviews or at public events.

22. Ronald Fernandez, Serafin Mendez Mendez, and Gaile, *Puerto Rico Past and Present: An Encyclopedia*, Greenwood Press, (Westport, Conn.: 19tK), 48, where they discuss the so-called blood tax. They also cite Luis R. Davila Conon, "The Blood Tax: The Puerto Rican Contribution to the United States War Effort," *Revista del Colegio de Abogados de Puerto Rico*, November 1979, 603-40; several books have been written on the subject of Puerto Ricans in the U.S. military, and the issue has been the subject of considerable debate over the years within Puerto Rico.

23. Fernandez, Mendez Mendez, and Cueto, *Puerto Rico Past and Present*, 48.

24. From an article written by Prof. Jose Lopez, director of the Juan Antonio Corretger Puerto Rican Cultural Center in Chicago, Illinois, entitled "To Act Upon the World and Transform It: Puerto Ricans in the USA and the Building of Decolonizing Institutions," published in *Puerto Rico: The Cost of Colonialism* by the FOR Task Force on Latin America and the Caribbean, 1992.

25. In an interview by the author with Governor Pedro Roselló in his office in 1998, he went as far as saying this "military service has been a great honor for Puerto Ricans in their role in defending the national security of the United States," but that it has been "spoiled by the ongoing colonial relationship which has never really recognized the sacrifice of Puerto Ricans."

26. I should point out that I never refer to the United States as the "mainland," a term used again and again even in progressive circles, because of its implied acceptance of the colonial status quo and the tendency to create a political imbalance between the large territory of the forty-eight contiguous states and the small islands that make up Puerto Rico. Throughout the years in my radio programs and writings, I always refer to the mainland as Puerto Rico, in reference to mainland Puerto Rico, as opposed to the islands of Vieques, Culebra, and Mono which make up the Puerto Rican archipelago. In referring to the United States, I simply say "the United States."

27. See Juan R. Torruella, *The Supreme Court and Puerto Rico: The Doctrine of Separate and Unequal* (San Juan, PR: Editorial de la Universidad de Puerto Rico, 1988), for a thorough examination of the so-called Insular cases that ostensibly laid the foundation for the current status of the island.

28. See Trias Monge, *Puerto Rico*, where he discusses the failed solutions proposed by Washington to the status question throughout the book.

29. Morales Carrion, *Puerto Rico*, 221-23; plus many other histories about Albizu. See also Juan Manuel Garcia Passalacqua, *Puerto Rico Equality and Freedom at Issue*, (New York: Praeger, 1984); and

Juan Angel Silen, *Pedro Albizu Campos* (Río Piedra, P.R.: Editorial Antillana, 1976).

30. See Ronald Fernandez, *Prisoners of Colonialism: The Struggle for Justice in Puerto Rico*, (Monroe, ME: Common Courage Press, 1994), 17-57; Morales Carrion, *Puerto*, 221-223.

31. See Juan Angel Silen, *Pedro Albizu Campos*, where the author explains in great detail the varying emotions people feel when they think about Albizu. However, in the end, the nationalist leader is seen as a hero for Puerto Ricans. One example of the universal appreciation of Puerto Ricans for Albizu was seen at the 2000 National Puerto Rican Day Parade held in New York City, the largest annual gathering of Latinos anywhere in the country. The parade organizers dedicated the parade to Albizu, along with the struggle of the people of Vieques. This was seen as a major development, given the history of how independence advocates had been ostracized for years at the very mainstream event.

32. See Fernadez, Mendez Mendez, and Cueto, *Puerto Rico Past and Present*, pg. 215, where they discuss *La Mordaza*, or the gag law, which criminalized any activity that advocated the overthrow of the colonial government in Puerto Rico, i.e., the United States. As they point out, the law was passed about two years before any of the nationalists' armed actions against the United States, so it was not a measure against what today is popularly called terrorism.

33. For a very thorough examination of the ongoing status debate and the efforts to resolve the issue, see Trias Monge, *Puerto Rico*.

34. Roselló, interview.

35. Rubén Berriós Martínez, interview by author, February 1998, San Juan, Puerto Rico. Portions of this interview were broadcast on the Pacifica Radio documentary *Puerto Rico: Reflections on the Oldest Colony*.

36. Ibid.

37. Carlos Vizcarondon, interview by author, San Juan, Puerto Rico, May 1998.

38. From floor debate in the U.S. House of Representatives, March 22, 1998, considering the United States-Puerto Rico Political Status Act, introduced by Representative Donald Young, 104th Cong., September 30, 1996.

39. Roselló, interview.

40. In an interview by author on WBAI's *Wake-Up Call* (January 5, 2001), Dr. Palmira Ríos, special assistant to the dean of the International Studies Program at the University of Puerto Rico in Río Piedras, said the plebiscito criollo was nothing but a show by Roselló that set back the push to resolve the status question.

41. From "Aprueban resolución libre determinación para la Isla," EFE, July 12, 2000.

42. Ibid.

43. Professor Mendez was quoted in Benjamín Torres Gotay, "Fórmula esperanzadora para muchos," *El Nuevo Día*, July 12, 2000.

44. Ibid.

45. See Trias Monge, *Puerto Rico*, 185-86; only 19 percent of the Puerto Rican population can speak English with relative ease; 23 percent speak with relative difficulty; 58 percent speak only Spanish. In the wake of the inauguration of Governor Sila Maria Calderón in January 2001, the Puerto Rican Independence Party, through its senator Fernando Martín, introduced legislation in the Puerto Rican legislature to overturn the law passed under Roselló's administration that made Spanish and English the official languages of Puerto Rico. The law, if approved, would make Spanish once again the official language of the island. Leila Andreu Cuevas, trans.,"Reclaman reinstauración del español como único idioma official," (*El Diario/ La Prensa*, January 4, 2001).

46. See Trias Monge, *Puerto Rico*, for a thorough discussion of these debates. Also, Juan Gonzalez, *Harvest of Empire*, for a compelling look at the Puerto Rican reality today, making it totally unique vis-á-vis other immigrant communities.

47. While many people write this off as an insignificant factor in this unipolar era of U.S. global military hegemony, it is still something worth noting in terms of the ongoing discussions over Puerto Rico's status. For more on how the issue of the military in Puerto Rico was dealt with at the UN, see Fernandez, *Disenchanted Island*, 236-39.

48. See "The Updated United States-Puerto Rico Political Status Act," *Congressional Record*, House of Representatives, 104th Cong., 2nd sess., Sept. 30, 1996.

49. Juan Mari Bras, interview by author, Mayaguez, Puerto Rico, March 24, 1998.

50. Luis Nieves Falcon, interview by author, Puerto Rico, February, 1998.

51. From "Aprueban resolución libre."

52. From the television documentary *Vieques: The Island and Its People*, hosted by Joe Sanchez and produced by Vicente Juarbe for broadcast on the *Dos Mundos* series on public station WPVI-TV, 1982.

53. From the same documentary, presenting a clip from *ABC News*, recorded from WAPA-TV, November 1979.

54. Sociologist Emilio Pantojas, chair of the Center for Caribbean Studies at the University of Puerto Rico, Rio Piedras, used this term in describing the action, during a WBAI interview, May 5, 2000.

55. From Humberto Garcia Muniz, "U.S. Military Installations in Puerto Rico: Controlling the Caribbean," in *Colonial Dilemma: Critical Perspectives on Contemporary Puerto Rico*, (Boston: South End Press, 1993).

56. Ibid. 54.

57. Ibid. 55.

58. From the radio documentary, *Puerto Rico: Reflections on the Oldest Colony*, produced by myself after several visits to the island in 1998. This section was taken directly from her Carambot's testimony at the town hall meeting. I also interviewed her extensively later.

59. From a copy of the letter made available to me by Ramon Rodriguez through David Cline, a member of Vietnam Veterans for Vieques, who went to the island as part of a delegation of veterans who opposed the ongoing bombing tests on Vieques. A number of other residents showed me similar letters that contained the same contents with their names handwritten at the top.

60. Garcia Muniz, "U.S. Military Installations," in *Colonial Dilemma: Critical Perspectives on Contemporary Puerto Rico*, South End Press, Boston, 1993.

61. Ibid., 61.

62. Leonor Mulero, *El Nuevo Dia*, "Sigue relegada la transferencia de las tierras en Vieques," July13, 2000.

63. From author interview, which aired on the radio documentary *Puerto Rico: Reflections*; this sentiment was echoed repeatedly by numerous navy and Pentagon officials, as well as lawmakers, such as Sen. James Inhofe, chairman of the Senate Select Committee on Military Preparedness, during the controversy in the wake of the death of David Sanes.

64. Neftali Garcia, interview by author, San Juan, February 1998. Scientific and Technical Services has a number of studies available. Their telephone number is 787-759-8787.

65. Carlos Ventura, interview by author, Vieques, Puerto Rico, March 1998. Part of this interview was broadcast on *Puerto Rico: Reflections*, on Pacifica Radio.

66. Winston Martinez, interview by author, Roosevelt Roads Naval Station, La Ceiba, Puerto Rica, March 1998. Parts of this interview were broadcast on *Puerto Rico: Reflections*, on Pacifica Radio.

67. From a speech given by Dr. Rafael Rivera Castano in New York City at the Brecht Forum, June 1998, sponsored by NACLA, WBAI's *Our Americas*, and the War Resisters League. For specific details on the various cancer studies done on Vieques, visit the Vieques Libre website at www.viequeslibre.org.

68. Dr. Doug Rokke, interview by author, March 13, 2000. *Our Americas.*

69. From a letter to Puerto Rico's secretary of health, Carmen Melecio, from the NRC's Luis Reyes, dated February 1, 2000, made available to author by Dr. Rokke.

70. Chris Hawley, "NRC, Activists Clash on Cleanup," Associated Press, June 7, 2000.

71. "UN Reports Finding Radioactivity at Sampled Sites in Kosovo Struck By NATO Munitions," Reuters, January 6, 2001.

72. Rokke, interview, interview *Our Americas*, May 23, 2000.

73. Reuters, January 29, 2000; Associated Press, January 29, 2000.

74. From a written press statement issued by Dr. Doug Rokke, February 9, 2000.

75. Camile Roldan Soto, "La Marina le cierra el paso a Robert Kennedy," *El Nuevo Dia*, June 19, 2000.

76. "Navy Bombarded with Suits," Associated Press, June 16, 2000.

77. Puerto Rican resident commissioner Carlos Romero Barcelo, a former governor and now the island's only (nonvoting) representative in the U.S. Congress, used these terms to describe the protesters the day after they were arrested in an interview with the author on WBAI's *Wake-Up Call*, May 5, 2000.

78. Falvio Cumpiano, interview by author, *Our Americas*, Pacifica Radio, May 5, 2000.

79. Carlos Romero Barcelo, interview by author, WBAI, *Wake Up Call*, May 5, 2000.

80. Leila Andreu Cuevas, "Altas expectativas en los primeros 100 Días," *El Diario/La Prensa*, January 3, 2001.

81. Dr. Palmira Ríos, special assistant to the dean of the International Studies Program, University of Puerto Rico, interview by author, *Wake-Up Call*, WBAI, January 5, 2001.

82. From *Environmental Assessment for the Relocation of Special Operations Command, South and Selected U.S. Army South Elements from the Republic of Panama to U.S. Naval Station Roosevelt Roads and Other Locations*, prepared for U.S. Army South and SOC-SOUTH by U.S. Army Corps of Engineers, December 1998.

83. "Puerto Rico Becoming a Military Hub for U.S.," *Miami Herald*, July 6, 1999.

84. "Miedo al contagio narco-guerrillero y a desplazados," *El Tiempo* (Colombia), August 23, 2000.

85. "Counter-Drug Implications of the U.S. Leaving Panama," testimony from Ana Maria Salazar, deputy assistant secretary of defense for drug enforcement policy and support, U.S. House of Representatives Committee on Government Reform, Subcommittee on Criminal Justice, Drug Policy, and Human Resources, June 9, 2000.

86. Carmelo Ruiz Marrero. "La estructura del comando sur," posted on the viequeslibre.org website, June 2, 2000; see also "ROTHR: Un Radar Militar Que No Combate el Narcotráfico," *Frente Unido Pro-Defensa del Valle de Lajas*, (Lajas, Puerto Rico), 1998.

87. For one of the most thorough collections of this kind of reporting, especially during the early days of U.S. colonial control, see Fernandez, *Disenchanted Island*.

MARIO ALFONSO MURILLO is an Assistant Professor of Communication at Hofstra University, and teaches media classes at New York University and the Autonomous University of Asuncion in Paraguay. He is host and producer of the weekly radio program *Our Americas*, a joint production of WBAI in New York and the North American Congress on Latin America (NACLA), distributed nationally by Pacifica Radio. He reports regularly for *Latino USA*, National Public Radio, and Pacifica's *Democracy Now*, and has written about Latin America and the Caribbean for a number of publications, including *El Diario La Prensa*, *In These Times*, *Urban: The Latino Magazine*, *New York Latino*, *Native Americas* and *NACLA Report on the Americas*.

OTHER TITLES IN THE OPEN MEDIA PAMPHLET SERIES

CORPORATE MEDIA
AND THE THREAT TO DEMOCRACY
Robert W. McChesney
80 pages / $5.95 / ISBN: 1-888363-47-9

MEDIA CONTROL:
THE SPECTACULAR ACHIEVEMENTS
OF PROPAGANDA
Noam Chomsky
64 pages / $5.95 / ISBN: 1-888363-49-5

GENE WARS:
THE POLITICS OF BIOTECHNOLOGY
Kristin Dawkins
64 pages / $4.95 / ISBN: 1-888363-48-7

GLOBALIZING CIVIL SOCIETY:
RECLAIMING OUR RIGHT TO POWER
David C. Korten
80 pages / $5.95 / ISBN: 1-888363-59-2

ZAPATISTA ENCUENTRO:
DOCUMENTS FROM THE 1996 ENCOUNTER FOR
HUMANITY AGAINST NEOLIBERALISM
The Zapatistas
64 pages / $5.95 / ISBN: 1-888363-58-4

PROPAGANDA INC.:
SELLING AMERICA'S CULTURE TO THE WORLD
Nancy Snow
64 pages / $5.95 / ISBN: 1-888363-74-6

A SUSTAINABLE ECONOMY FOR THE
21ST CENTURY
Juliet Schor
64 pages / $5.95 / ISBN: 1-888363-75-4

THE PROGRESSIVE GUIDE TO ALTERNATIVE
MEDIA AND ACTIVISM
Project Censored
128 pages / $10.00 / ISBN: 1-888363-84-3

THE UMBRELLA OF U.S. POWER
Noam Chomsky
80 pages / $5.95 / ISBN: 1-888363-85-1

MICRORADIO AND DEMOCRACY:
(LOW) POWER TO THE PEOPLE
Greg Ruggiero
64 pages / $5.95 / ISBN: 1-58322-000-3

POEMS FOR THE NATION:
A COLLECTION OF CONTEMPORARY
POLITICAL POEMS
Allen Ginsberg, with Eliot Katz and Andy Clausen
80 pages / $5.95 / ISBN: 1-58322-012-7

THE CASE AGAINST LAME DUCK
IMPEACHMENT
Bruce Ackerman
80 pages / $8.00 / ISBN: 1-58322-004-6

ACTS OF AGGRESSION:
POLICING "ROGUE" STATES
Noam Chomsky, Ramsey Clark, Edward W. Said
64 pages / $6.95 / ISBN: 1-58322-005-4

THE LAST ENERGY WAR:
THE BATTLE OVER UTILITY DEREGULATION
Harvey Wasserman
80 pages / $5.95 / ISBN: 1-58322-017-8

IT'S THE MEDIA, STUPID
John Nichols and Robert W. McChesney
128 pages / $10.00 / ISBN: 1-58322-029-1

CUTTING CORPORATE WELFARE
Ralph Nader
144 pages / $10.00 / ISBN: 1-58322-033-X

THE WTO: FIVE YEARS OF REASONS TO RESIST
CORPORATE GLOBALIZATION
Lori Wallach and Michelle Sforza
Introduction by Ralph Nader
80 pages / $5.95 / ISBN: 1-58322-035-6

THE CASE OF MUMIA ABU-JAMAL:
A LIFE IN THE BALANCE
Amnesty International
64 pages / $6.95 / ISBN: 1-58322-081-X

WEAPONS IN SPACE
Karl Grossman
80 pages / $6.95 / ISBN: 1-58322-044-5

**TO ORDER ADDITIONAL TITLES IN THE
OPEN MEDIA PAMPHLET SERIES
CALL 1 (800) 596-7437, OR
VISIT WWW.SEVENSTORIES.COM**